# Brain Movies:
## The Original Teleplays of
# Harlan Ellison®

## Volume Six

AN EDGEWORKS ABBEY OFFERING

BRAIN MOVIES
THE ORIGINAL TELEPLAYS OF HARLAN ELLISON®
VOLUME SIX
is an Edgeworks Abbey® offering in association with Jason Davis.
Published by arrangement with the Author and The Kilimanjaro Corporation.

BRAIN MOVIES
THE ORIGINAL TELEPLAYS OF HARLAN ELLISON®
VOLUME SIX

Harlan Ellison website: www.HarlanEllison.com
To order books: www.HarlanEllisonBooks.com

Editor:   Jason Davis

Assistant Editor:   Cynthia Davis

Designer:   Bo Nash

ISBN: 978-0-9895257-6-3

FIRST EDITION

Special thanks to Steve Barber.

Copyright acknowledgments appear on page 241, which constitutes an extension of this copyright page.

17082014

This book is dedicated to the
nonpareil wit and memory
of my friend,

LENNY BRUCE

# nota bene:

The documents in this book were reproduced from the author's file copies. They originated on a manual typewriter, hence the idiosyncrasies that set them apart from the sanitized, word-processed pages of today. The progressive lightening of the text followed by a sudden darkening of the same, indicates the author has changed the typewriter's ribbon; it is *not* a printing defect.

Throughout the works presented herein, there is evidence of the author's revision: struck-out text, handwritten emendations, and typewritten text printed over passages that were cancelled with correcting tape. These artifacts have been maintained to preserve the evidence of the writer's process.

# Contents

Who Killed ½ of Glory Lee?

### Editor's Note: One For the Great Stone Face

"I came to be very fond of Gene Barry," recalls Ellison of the actor who played Amos Burke, the eponymous millionaire LAPD Homicide captain of *Burke's Law*. "He was a gentleman, had a great voice, and could say any line I wrote. He subsequently went on to do *La Cage Aux Folles* on Broadway, and was magnificent in it."

Of Barry's co-stars, Ellison said, "Regis Toomey was a great character actor, so I would make sure that he got some minutes on screen because I loved his act. Gary Conway—who played Tim Tilson—was the Fred to Barry's Super Chicken. Whenever Gene was off shooting, you would write a scene for Gary—who was not Ronald Colman or Paul Muni—but was a perfectly workable, hard-working, polite, good guy who never flubbed lines and always hit his mark, which is all Jimmy Stewart said you had to do to be employable."

For his fourth and final episode of the series, Ellison turned to "the world of *shmatte*, as we say in Yiddish; that is to say 'cloak-and-suit.' (My people always say 'cloak-and-suit,' which is where most publishers started—on Sixth or Seventh Avenue, in the Garment District in New York—then they became hotsy-totsy publishers.)"

Ellison wrote the part of Anjanette Delecroix in the hopes of landing a French guest star for the role. "In this case, it was Nina Foch, who had not the best French accent, but then neither was Dick Van Dyke's—in *Mary Poppins*—the best cockney accent in the world."

"Who Killed ½ of Glory Lee?" aired on the 8th of May 1964, the final installment of *Burke's Law*'s freshman season on ABC. The series would have one more year before the success of the James Bond movies and NBC's *The Man From U.N.C.L.E.* (for which Ellison would script two segments in the 1966–7 season, both in BRAIN MOVIES, Volume 2) convinced the suits to abandon police procedurals, re-christening the series *Amos Burke, Secret Agent* for one disastrous season. But Ellison wouldn't be back for Burke's second sally onto the primetime schedule; his welcome at ABC had been deep-sixed by Adrian Samish (whose foul stench also wafts through BRAIN MOVIES, Volumes 2, 3, and 5).

Dubious accents and network machinations aside, for Ellison, the highlight of "Glory Lee" was another of the show's trademark guest stars: "When you go to your grave, what better can you say than 'I wrote for Buster Keaton once'? He was superlative. He was elderly at the time, but still mesmerizing." The role—which Ellison crafted as an *hommage* to silent-era icon's *œuvre*—would prove to be one of his last.

## "WHO KILLED ½ OF GLORY LEE?"

FADE IN:

1    INT. ELLISON BUILDING   ESTABLISHING SHOT   LOBBY   MORNING

EXTREME CLOSEUP on a shapely pair of female legs as a skirt
is raised just above the knees.

> BARBY'S VOICE O.S.
> Now I ask you, in all fairness; what have
> these models got that I haven't got?

During speech CAMERA PULLS BACK to show BARBY and TWO OTHER
GIRLS, all dressed in the uniforms of elevator operators;
as they stand talking the Building comes to life around
them: several other elevator girls pass them, a STARTER--
regal in mufti and whistle--checks controls for the bank
of elevators in a control box on one wall, an old walrus-
mustachioed NIGHT WATCHMAN packs up his possessions and
begins to move his sign-in book and watchstand-podium.

The Building has a huge lobby, marble-tiled (if possible)
and sports a long line of elevators along one wall.

> 1ST GIRL
> (to Barby)
> Well, for openers, Barby, they've got
> jobs.

> BARBY
> (drops skirt)
> So? I've got a job, too. You think
> if I was a ward of the state I'd be
> developing nose-bleeds running an
> elevator?

> 2nd GIRL
> Ah-ha! That is the difference. You
> run the elevator in a building where
> beautiful women come in six-paks.

> 1st GIRL
> You've got the right dream, sweetie,
> but the wrong location.

(CONTINUED)

3

1    CONTINUED:

> 2nd GIRL
> There're thirty-five high fashion
> manufacturers in this building, and each
> one has half a dozen models...

> 1st GIRL
> Which makes roughly two hundred and ten
> swingers cutting your chances, Sweetie.

> 2nd GIRL
> Which leaves you about as much chance
> as a snail in a bucket of salt.

While conversation ensues, secretaries, businessmen and
attractive models with hatboxes have begun to appear, and
enter the elevators in motion.  The Starter's whistle has
sounded shrilly several times, and now he moves to them.

> STARTER
> Okay, you girls.  Move it.  Get those
> cages working.

The girls move toward their elevators.

> BARBY
> (ruefully)
> Big Brother is watching.

2  ·  TRUCKING SHOT    WITH BARBY

as she moves to her elevator, the only one still closed
and not working.  She inserts her long handle-key in the
slot at the side of the door, but it won't turn.  She
struggles with it a moment, as the Starter, who has been
watching, stalks over to her.

> STARTER
> Now what's slowing you down?

> BARBY
> (irritably)
> It won't unlock.  Car must be abovefloors.

Starter looks up.  CAMERA RISES to floor indicator.  The
arrow is at 5.

> STARTER
> Cage seems to be stuck on the fifth
> floor.  I'll check the controls.

He moves toward the control box on the wall.  CAMERA
GOES WITH HIM.

3    REVERSE ANGLE

PAST STARTER as the SOUND of a terrible rushing fills the
lobby.  The SOUND OF A FALLING ELEVATOR...shrieking of metal,
roaring of a great weight coming down.  CAMERA ZOOMS IN
RAPIDLY on terrified face of Barby as she spins toward the
Starter, and PAST HER, RISING to the indicator arrow as it
spins around and around madly.  CAMERA PULLS BACK RAPIDLY
as the SOUND of the cage CRASHING shakes lobby and CAMERA

Everyone stops in their tracks, frozen in horror.

                    BARBY
          It fell!  It fell from the fifth
          floor.

The Starter rushes back to her, and the closed door.

                    STARTER
                    (panicing)
          We've got to get it open...if there
          was anyone in that car...

Barby re-inserts her lock-key and they try to shove the door
open.  It is wedged shut.

                    STARTER
                    (continues;
                    over shoulder)
          Hey!  Give me a hand here, will you!

Several businessmen in grey flannel, with attache cases,
rush to his aid.  They all apply weight to shoving the door.
It begins to slide back in its tracks.  CAMERA MOVES IN on
their straining bodies...then suddenly, the door gives, and
slams all the way open.
                                        HARD CUT TO:

4    INT. ELEVATOR CAR  DAY

EXTREME CLOSEUP on a face as it falls toward CAMERA; PANS
WITH the face as the body falls forward and HOLDS TIGHT on
the body as it falls stiffly, arms at sides, to the floor,
and CAMERA CLOSEUP as the face actually shatters, sending
bits and pieces skittering across the tiles.  The SOUND of
a scream from Barby as the dress dummy falls past her.

CAMERA TILTS UP into car and PANS SLOWLY ACROSS a tangled
jungle of smashed dress dummies in grotesque, contorted
positions, arms upflung, legs twisted off, wide staring
faces empty of life, a Grand Guignol of pseudo-humans.
As CAMERA PANS ACROSS, one face--a man--seems somehow
odder than the rest of the dummies, but CAMERA GOES PAST,
then stops, PANS RAPIDLY BACK and ZOOMS IN to show us it
is not just another dress dummy.
                                        (CONTINUED)

4    CONTINUED:

It is a man.  A dead man, with a crushed skull, slumped in
among the jammed-together dress dummies.  CAMERA PULLS
QUICKLY BACK to include Barby whose SCREAM is cut off as
she tries to force her hand into her mouth and a simultaneous

                                        SHARP CUT TO:

5    INT. AMOS' STUDY   ESTABLISHING   MORNING

EXTREME CLOSEUP on another hand.  A poker hand.  And four
other pairs of hands holding cards across a round poker table.

                        AMOS' VOICE O.S.
                    (as other hand tosses
                      chips into pot)
            I'll see you...and bump you five. Satch?

CAMERA RISES to show us AMOS BURKE, who has obviously been
at this game through the long, sleepless night.  There is
a faint grey patina of beard on his cheeks, his tuxedo tie
is undone, and he looks beat.  He pulls deeply at his LAM
and exhales a thick plume of atmospheric smoke as CAMERA
TRAVELS RIGHT to the next player, a gorgeous redhead SATCH.
She wears a green gambler's eyeshade, a jarring note with
her decollète evening gown.

                        SATCH
                    (scrutinizing hand)
            Not with this chicken salad.  I fold.
            How about you, Lefty?

CAMERA TRAVELS RIGHT to next player.  LEFTY is an incredibly
constructed blonde whose puff sleeves are held up by gambler
sleeve-garters.  She wears dark glasses.

                        LEFTY
                    (tossing in chips)
            Ante, Amos' raise and ten more just
            to keep things interesting.  Whaddaya
            say, Doc?

CAMERA TRAVELS RIGHT to DOC, a stunning brunette with a
cigarette in the corner of her mouth, and her cards close
to her impressive chest.

                        DOC
            Mmmm.  I'll pony up.
                    (chips in)
            It's all up to you, Tiger.

                                    (CONTINUED)

5    CONTINUED:

CAMERA TRAVELS RIGHT to Tiger, who is none other than our
old friend HENRY, with a massive stack pile of chips in front
of him.  Henry throws in his fifteen chips.

                HENRY
I'm in.  See Boss' raise, and Miss
Lefty, ten.  Moment of truth at hand.
         (lays down cards)
Straight to King.

The others throw in their hands.

                AMOS
That beats my bullets.  Where did you
learn to hustle poker, Henry?

                HENRY
        (raking in chips)
Strange power I acquire in Orient, where
I also pick up ability to cloud men's
minds.

                SATCH
Very funny, Lamont Cranston.  I'm out
a bundle.

                DOC
What time is it?

                AMOS
        (consults watch)
Close to nine o'clock.

                DOC
        (gathering, shuffling
           cards)
Ayem or peeyem?

                AMOS
        (wearily)
A.M.  We've been at it all night.

                LEFTY
I used to think there was only one nine
o'clock...the one at night.  You're
having a corrupting influence on me,
Amos.

                AMOS
This game was you girls idea, not mine.

                SATCH
We had to get it settled once and for all,
who you belong to.

Brain Movies

6    ANOTHER ANGLE    THE SCENE   AMOS IN F.G.

>                AMOS
> Yes, but playing cards for me...it
> makes me feel like...like...<u>property</u>!

>                LEFTY
> Better <u>you</u> should feel uncomfortable
> than <u>us</u>.  Common brawling ain't ladylike.

>                DOC
> And I keep running my nylons, knife-
> fighting over you.

>                AMOS
> All right, cut out the funnies.  Let's
> call off this ridiculous game.

>                SATCH
> Too late now.  Heavy winner gets you;
> and besides, your sidekick here has used
> everything but a vacuum cleaner on us.

>                HENRY
> Perfectly happy to keep money, let you
> ladies fight over Boss.

>                AMOS
> Thanks.  Traitor.

>                DOC
> Your own fault for being so much in
> demand, Captain Burkesir.

>                AMOS
>              (sheepishly)
> But...but...I'm not that kind of boy.
> I mean...this could spoil a fellahs
> reputation.

This reversal of the Standard Female Line makes each of
them start with surprise.  They all do takes as phone
RINGS.  Henry reaches under table, pulls up receiver.

>                HENRY
> Dirty Eddie's Poker Parlor, Henry speaking.
>              (He listens, hands
>               receiver to Amos)
> It for you, Dirty Eddie.

Amos gives him a scathing look, yanks receiver away.

7    CLOSEUP    AMOS ON PHONE

> AMOS
> Good morning, Tim.  No, I wasn't
> sleeping.  What've you got?
> (beat)
> Killed in an elevator crash?  So why
> homicide?
> (beat)
> It was tampered with?  What's the
> address?  The Ellison Building...that's
> in the heart of the garment district,
> right?  Give me twenty-five minutes.

He hangs up receiver as CAMERA PULLS BACK to full shot.

> AMOS
> (continues)
> (to Henry)
> Okay, Diamond Jim, cash in and let's
> hit the street.

> DOC
> You're leaving.

> AMOS
> You've got a lightning mind there, Doc.

> LEFTY
> Hold it, pardner, nobody leaves when I'm
> losing.

> HENRY
> Nobody like sore loser.

> AMOS
> (to Henry)
> Get them a pot of coffee and a fresh
> deck.  And a change of clothes for me.
> (to girls)
> Game called onaccounta murder.

> SATCH
> We'll wait, play a little three-handed
> stud till you get back.  The question
> of your ownership should be settled by
> then.

> AMOS
> (rising)
> To the victor belongs the spoils.

(CONTINUED)

7    CONTINUED:

Amos turns and starts to walk toward door as Doc's voice
stops him.

                         DOC'S VOICE O.S.
              We'll call her; see if she wants to play.

Amos turns, confused.

                         AMOS
              Who?

                         DOC
                       (wryly)
              Victor.

Eyes heavenward, staggering mentally, Amos resumes his exit.

                                        CUT TO:

8    EXT. AMOS' HOUSE (STOCK)    DAY

as Amos emerges, followed by Henry with street clothes on
hanger; Amos shrugging into tuxedo jacket, tie still loose,
they enter car, as we flash

                    MAINTITLES

Rolls spins out of driveway, into street.

9    PROGRESS SHOTS  STREET (STOCK)  DAY

as MAINTITLES CONTINUE OVER, the Rolls buzzes merrily along.

                                        FADE OUT.


              (COMMERCIAL INSERT)


     FADE IN:

10   INT. ROLLS  DAY

CLOSEUP on back seat utility shelf, an electric coffee pot
perking, a mirror propped up and an electric razor being
picked up by Amos.

11   REVERSE ANGLE   AMOS & TIM    DAY

Tim sits beside Amos, reading from notes while Amos starts
to shave.  He now wears a fresh shirt, a four-in-hand tie
with knot slipped down so he can shave.

                                        (CONTINUED)

11    CONTINUED:

> TIM
> Someone smashed the safety mechanism
> with a ball-pein (peen) hammer.  We
> found it on the fifth floor.

> AMOS
> I thought it was impossible for one
> of those cages to tumble.

> TIM
> It is, on the new ones.  But they
> remodeled the building about sixteen
> years ago and someone got cheapo when
> it came to replacing the elevators.
> (beat)
> New interiors for the cars, but the
> same old mechanisms.  There's an
> elevator inspector somewhere getting
> fat on payola.

> AMOS
> (sarcastically)
> Sounds like the biggest scandal since
> the Teapot Dome.  What else have you
> got?

> TIM
> (reading)
> His name was Benjamin Glory, age 51,
> and until that cage fell, he was an
> extraordinarily healthy specimen.
> (beat)
> He was half-owner of a very exclusive
> high fashion coutourier. Glory Lee Frocks.

Amos finishes shaving, applies lotion, slips tie knot up
and shrugs into street jacket as Tim helps.

> AMOS
> Half?

> TIM
> The surviving partner's name is KeeKee Lee.

> AMOS
> Hmmm.  Who Killed One-Half of Glory Lee.
> (beat)
> Come on, we'll play detective.

12    EXT. ELLISON BUILDING   STREET   DAY

a HIGH MEDIUM SHOT down on Amos and Tim as they emerge from
Rolls and walk across sidewalk toward building.  It is a
large, impressive many-storeyed building (at least seven
floors).  They enter building.

                                        RAPID DISSOLVE TO:

13    INT. LOBBY   ELLISON BUILDING    DAY

MEDIUM CLOSEUP over shoulder of Amos as he stares at a
series of bronze plaques on a marble wall.  The plaques read:

    HENRI PARIS SPORTSWEAR     HIGHSTYLE, INC.    GLORY LEE FROCKS
    BETTINA CASUALS    FUTURAMA BRASSIERES    MISS JUDY DRESSES

CAMERA PULLS BACK as Tim moves in beside Amos.

                    TIM
          There's something special about this
          kill, Captain.

                    AMOS
          Something special about all of them.

                    TIM
          But this time it'll make your hair
          stand on end.

                    AMOS
          You've been brainwashed by The Beatles.
                    (beat)
          Let's say my hair stays where it is...
          what's the twist in this problem?

                    TIM
          I'll let Les tell you; we disagree on
          theory.

                    AMOS
          Don't feel badly; they snickered at
          Da Vinci, they laughed at Galileo, they
          said Kleinsfogel was a lunatic.

                    TIM
          Kleinsfogel?  Who was Kleinsfogel?

                    AMOS
                 (walking away)
          A lunatic.

14    ANGLE ON MURDER ELEVATOR

as Amos approaches, LESTER HART comes to meet him; as Les
approaches, he gives ad lib instructions to a harness bull,
claps him on the shoulder and the cop goes off to perform
the chore.  We can see into the elevator, at the clutch of
blind-staring dummies.  Technicians work on the cage and its
contents, dusting for prints; a sheet-covered body on a
rolling stretcher is being hustled out of the cage by two
interns.  The Starter and his girls stand off to one side,
waiting. Les' first words are to Tim as he comes up with Amos.

                    LES
                 (to Tim)
          You're nuts.

                    AMOS
           I already told him.  What seems to
           be gnawing at you, Intrepid Sergeant
           Hart?

The body starts past, being pushed by interns.  Les stops
them, flips back the sheet for Amos to look.

                    AMOS
                 (continues)
           Nasty.  Like someone dropped a watermelon
           off the roof.

Les flips sheet back, nods the interns on their way.  He
turns back to Amos.

                    LES
           See those clothing dummies?
                 (Amos nods)
           Okay.  Now picture that car full of people,
           real people, instead of mannequins, which is
           the way it should have been.

                    AMOS
           I'm picturing.

                    LES
           The killer had no way of knowing that car
           wasn't full of people, going down for
           coffee or something.  So when he dropped
           the cage, he was prepared to kill everyone
           in it.  We're lucky this Benjamin Glory
           was bringing down a stock of dummies or
           we'd have a lobbyful of corpses now.

                              (CONTINUED)

14    CONTINUED:

                    AMOS
You're getting positively ghoulish in
your old age, Les.
            (beat; to Tim)
And you disagree with the Good Sergeant's
theory, MR. KLEINSFOGEL?

                    TIM
Right.  I think whoever dumped that cage
knew Glory would be alone in it.

                    LES
Then how do you explain the fact that the
Glory Lee operation takes up the entire
sixth floor, but the elevator fell from
the fifth?

                    TIM
I uh haven't quite worked that out yet,
but ix it's a sounder theory than yours,
Les!  According to you, we've got a
homicidal mass murderer running loose.

                    LES
And I say it wasn't Glory the killer
was after!

                    AMOS
            (soothingly)
Gentlemen, gentlemen, restrain yourselves.
            (nods to Starter
            and girls)
We're being observed by taxpayers; we
don't want them to think we're confused,
do we?

At this point the Coroner, GEORGE McCLOUD walks over to
the group.  He nods to Amos.

                    McCLOUD
You look wretched; almost as bad as the
late Benjamin Glory.  Rough night?

                    AMOS
Poker game.

                    McCLOUD
            (to Tim & Les, archly)
And you had me believing those wild yarns
about his inherited wealth.  He's a common
card shark.

                                    (CONTINUED)

14

14     CONTINUED: - 2

                          AMOS
            Before you pick up your paycheck and
            leave under a cloud, McCloud, do you
            have any goodies for us?

                          McCLOUD
            Fractured skull, internal hemhorraging,
            bone splinters in the brain...he died
            from everything but hoof-and-mouth
            disease.  Maybe there'll be more later,
            but that was definitely the cause of
            death.

                          AMOS
            You're certain.  I don't want another
            one of those winners where you tell
            us he drowned, and we find out later
            he was run over by a midget on a tricycle.

                          McCLOUD
            I'm certain.  If he didn't die in that
            crash I'll go back to being a veterinanian.
                          (beat)
            But here's something you can play with.

He digs through a large manila envelope, comes up with
a small piece of metal.  Hands it to Amos.

                          McCLOUD
                          (continues)
            This was in his pocket.  The rest is all
            standard personal effects.

15     INTERCUT    THE INSIGNIA

It is the gold eagle of a Colonel in the US Army, off an
officer's dress uniform, shoulder insignia.

                          AMOS' VOICE O.S.
            A colonel's insignia, a gold eagle, US
            Army.

16     ANOTHER ANGLE    THE GROUP

                          McCLOUD
            And on that mysterious note I bid you
            fond adieu.  I'll be in touch when I
            have more particulars.

He leaves.

17    MEDIUM SHOT   THE GROUP

PAST Amos and Tim and Les to NIGHT WATCHMAN as he comes
toward them out of the crowd.  He carries a lunch pail
and is a remarkable-looking old coot.  Something out of
American Gothic, perhaps, with walrus mustache.

                    NIGHT WATCHMAN
          Say...you the big honcho?

                    LES
          This is Captain Burke.  Amos, this is
          the Night Watchman.

                    NIGHT WATCHMAN
          Yeah, well, let's cut all the flapdoodle,
          and let me give you my clue so I can get
          the heck out of here.  I've got to be on
          TV in another two hours.

                    AMOS
          TV?

                    NIGHT WATCHMAN
          Yeah, I'm a contestant on the "Grab Or
          Get Out" quiz show.  Heck, I'm after
          my eleventh straight win today...that's
          the ninth plateau.  Got a chance to win
          twelve thousand, five hundred pounds of
          frozen Giant Wooly Mammoth Meat.
                    (beat)
          Now, you want my clue or not?

                    AMOS
                    (staggered)
          Why, uh, sure, yes...naturally.

                    NIGHT WATCHMAN
          Benjamin Glory.  He got here at 5:30
          this morning, and signed my book, and
          went upstairs...

                    TIM
          Fifth or sixth floor?

                    NIGHT WATCHMAN
          Sixth, o'course.  That's where the
          Glory Lee offices are.  He didn't have
          no reason to be on five.

Tim looks at Les smugly.  Les ignores it.

18    2-SHOT    AMOS & NIGHT WATCHMAN

                    AMOS
Did you see him again after he
went up to the sixth floor?

            NIGHT WATCHMAN
Nope.

                    AMOS
Did you see anyone else between the
time Glory arrived and the elevator
fell?

            NIGHT WATCHMAN
Nope.

                    AMOS
And that's the entire clue you have
for us?

            NIGHT WATCHMAN
Yep.  But it's your own fault.

                AMOS
              (quizzically)
Our fault?

            NIGHT WATCHMAN
Sure.  You ain't even offering a
consolation prize if I get wrong
answers.  You guys can't fool me...

                AMOS
              (puzzled)
Fool you...?

            NIGHT WATCHMAN
O'course.  You think I'm some kinda
dumbbell or something?  I know when
I'm on 'Candid Camera'.

He walks away.  They stare after, perplexedly.  Finally,
Tim speaks.

                TIM LES
So if the offices were all empty from
the night before, how did the killer
gain access to the building and to the
fifth floor so he could sabotage
that elevator?

                    TIM
Sixth floor.

19   ANOTHER SHOT   GROUP IN F.G.

as they have been standing there, a seemingly-endless
procession of incredible-looking models have been trooping
past, staring at them, and Amos (as well as Tim) have been
taking due note.

> AMOS
> (whistles)
> Time! Kindly Sergeant Hart feels the
> fifth floor is the proper place to
> begin our investigation.

> LES
> It's obvious...

> AMOS
> (continues)
> And Detective Tilson's current theory
> holds that Glory was the sole and only
> target, ergo, the sixth floor is the
> right way to go...

> TIM
> Well, logically...

> AMOS
> So we send you two to opposite corners.
> Les, clock the fifth floor. Tim, you
> come with me, and we'll talk to the other
> xxxxixing half   of Glory Lee.

They move toward another, waiting, elevator, and as they go,
they join a stream of pretty models with hatboxes also
heading for the elevator. There is brief flirtatious
interplay as Amos and Tim--and a beat later, Les--usher
the girls in gallantly.

> SOFT WIPE TO:

20   INT. SIXTH FLOOR HALLWAY   DAY

MEDIUM SHOT on double glass doors with legend GLORY LEE
FROCKS and EXCLUSIVE COUTURIÈRE in gold letters. The
models are going past, down the hall to another doorway
as Amos and Tim bid them adieu smilingly. Amos opens
door as CAMERA MOVES FORWARD THRU OPEN DOOR.

21   INT. GLORY LEE SHOWROOM   ESTABLISHING   DAY   AMOS' POV

WHAT HE SEES is a plush showroom with hanging silk folds,
deep modern sofas and seats, a small stage at the rear, a
number of drapery-hung doorways, several racks of clothes,
and dummies wearing high-fashion gowns. A number of very
beautiful girls stand around in posing attitudes.

> (CONTINUED)

21 CONTINUED:

To one side a PHOTOGRAPHER is setting up a fashion shot with
a beautiful model. The Photographer is also a woman, but
unlike the model in her sleek high fashion, she wears jeans
and a sweat shirt, albeit flattering to her figure. She is
all business, and a cigarette hangs from her lips.

Off to one side, a different scene is being played as CAMERA
PANS RIGHT to KEEKEE LEE and an old, dowdy but pixie-ish
woman, MRS. MACHREE (a Cheerio Meredith-type). KeeKee Lee
is long and slim and cool looking. The very epitome of the
high fashion world, in all ways a cool number. Except she
has the voice of a dock-walloper. She brandishes a flashy
silk dress at Mrs. Machree and shrieks at her viciously.

22 2-SHOT    MRS. MACHREE & KEEKEE LEE

                    KEEKEE
                 (viciously)
What an incredible clown you are!
What tapioca pudding you've got for
brains! Mrs. Machree, you're getting
senile, absolutely decrepit; I'm going
to have to shoot you like an old horse!

                    MRS. MACHREE
                 (timidly)
I'm only sixty-one, Miss Lee...

                    KEEKEE
Sixty-one is sixty more than you deserve!
Look at this number...it's ruined, positively
ruined...black smears all over it, matted
with foreign matter...it's a disgrace...

                    MRS. MACHREE
I didn't realize the steam iron was dirty...

                    KEEKEE
I pay you coolie wages to <u>notice</u> those
things, Mrs. Machree! What you deserve
is a stiff punch in the stomach...I'd
like to dribble you down the street like
a basketball...

23 INTERCUT  AMOS & TIM

as they stand in the still-open doorway, listening to
this tirade. The sound of ANOTHER BATTLE comes from another
direction.

24    PANNING SHOT   ACROSS SHOWROOM   RIGHT TO LEFT

from the scene of KeeKee Lee berating Mrs. Machree to a
similar scene, two women arguing, in a corner near an
alcove leading to a drapery-hung dressing room.  The
younger of the two women is incredibly beautiful, about
20 (this is vitally important, she must be no older) or
a little younger.  She is tall and slim and a stunner.
Her name is SABLE.  The other woman is older, perhaps
early forties, but lovely in a more demure, reserved, yet
electric way.  The older woman is ANJANETTE DELACROIX
(pronounced: Dehla-cr-wah).  They argue bitterly.  CAMERA
HOLDS on them as Anjanette grasps Sable's arm.

                    ANJANETTE
               (with slight, but
               noticeable, unidentifiable
                  accent)
          You're being a little fool!  I'm trying
          to save you...don't be so headstrong!

                    SABLE
               (furious)
          You're a witch, a miserable shrike!
          You know what a shrike is?  It's a bird
          that impales other birds on thorns...

                    ANJANETTE
          You're too young, you're only nineteen,
          how can you know what's best for you?
          I've been through it all, I know!

                    SABLE
          You won't let me live!  You want to
          run me!  But I'm not a toy.  So let me
          go...you old hag!

The older woman slaps Sable, who holds her face, begins
to cry.  The noise level mounts in the room, as the lady
photographer goes on about her business posing the models.

25    INTERCUT   SAME AS 23

Tim and Amos stare at each other, then move toward the
Photographer.  They walk up to her as she bends over her
tripod-rigged camera.  She straightens as they come up,
the cigarette still in the corner of her mouth.

                    PHOTOGRAPHER
          Welcome to the crowd scene from "Ben-Hur."

                                        (CONTINUED)

25    CONTINUED:

                         AMOS
              Do they always brawl like this?

                         PHOTOGRAPHER
              Does a kangaroo crave cumquats?

                         AMOS
              We haven't got a scorecard; mind identifying
              the players?

26    MEDIUM SHOT  PAST PHOTOGRAPHER

TO KEEKEE LEE & MRS. MACHREE as Photographer points.

                         PHOTOGRAPHER
              In the far corner, wearing the silk shantung
              sheath and twenty pounds of eye liner, is
              Miss KeeKee Lee, currently sole owner of
              Glory Lee Frocks.  Her opponent is the ever-
              popular bantamweight from the slave labor
              camp, Mrs. Ophelia Machree, wearing the
              renovated seed sack with whoopee socks and
              ankle-strap wedgies.

27    REVERSE ANGLE  PAST PHOTOGRAPHER

as she turns and points down the other way TO ANJANETTE
DELACROIX and SABLE, still arguing SOTTO VOCE.

                         PHOTOGRAPHER
              And in the near corner, cursing most
              foully in a phoney Swiss accent, is
              perennial crowd-pleaser, Mademoiselle
              Anjanette Delacroix, fashion designer
              of this sumptuous squirrel cage.  Her
              nimble adversary, the sexually-stimulating
              Sable Delacroix, her daughter, is decked
              out in the height of this season's
              fashion, what is known far and wide as
              "The Gentle Woman Look".  Lotsa luck.

She turns back to her camera, bends over and re-focuses.
Tim and Amos are left to their own devices.

                         AMOS
                    (pointing to left
                    and right, accordingly)
              I'll take the high road...
                    (points to KeeKee)
              and you take the low road...
                    (points to Sable)
              and I'll be in trouble before'ya.

They move apart, each in the proper direction.

NOTE: During the following scenes, intercutting between the
      two separate conversations provides a flow of infor-
mation, yet eliminates the static element of face-to-face
interrogation.  It is, in essence, two scenes being played
at the same time, with jumps from one conversation to the
other providing the linkage.

28   ANGLE  PAST KEEKEE LEE & MRS. MACHREE  TO AMOS

as he approaches them, they are still arguing.

                    KEEKEE
          Well, it's ruined...I might just as
          well tear it up and throw it out...

                 MRS. MACHREE
          I'll pay for it, Miss Lee!

                    KEEKEE
          Forty years it'd take you.  Forty years!
               (She hands her the
                ruined dress)
          Here, take the thing, it's yours.  Now get
          back to your ironing board!  Go on!

Amos reaches them.

                    AMOS
          Take it easy.  Mrs. Machree may be somebody's
          mother.

                    KEEKEE
          And who're you supposed to be?  The Court
          of Human Relations?

Amos flashes his tin.

                    AMOS
          Just call me a servant of the people...

                    KEEKEE
          Well, Mr. Servant, or Mr. People, or
          whoever you are, butt out.  I've got
          enough headaches today.

                    AMOS
          Headaches, you take aspirin; what do
          you suggest to cure murder?

KeeKee's look is one of fear.  She stares at Amos silently.
Mrs. Machree starts to edge away.  She pauses as she passes
Amos, murmurs a parting shot at him:

                                        (CONTINUED)

28    CONTINUED:

>                    MRS. MACHREE
>                      (sotto voce)
>            That "Mother" Machree jazz is pretty
>            square,  I expected better from you.

She vanishes through a drapery-hung archway as Amos' startled
expression follows her.

>                    KEEKEE
>            You mumbled "murder".  I suppose you
>            mean Benjamin's <u>accident</u> this morning.

>                    AMOS
>            Unless you're running a two-for-one sale
>            today, that's what I mean.

>                    KEEKEE
>            I repeat, Mr. uh--

>                    AMOS
>            Captain Amos Burke.  Homicide Division.

>                    KEEKEE
>                      (resuming)
>            ...ah! Well, Captain Burke, I repeat: an
>            accident, an unfortunate accident, but
>            by no stretch of the imagination, murder.

>                    AMOS
>                      (flat)
>            Someone sabotaged that elevator; we found
>            traces of tampering.  It was murder.

>                    KEEKEE
>            Ain't <u>that</u> a blast!  I always contended
>            Ben would go out the hard way, but if I'd
>            had to pick odds, I'd have voted he'd just
>            ugly away.

>                    AMOS
>            I understand you now own Glory Lee Frocks
>            entirely.

>                    KEEKEE
>            The usual "survivor clause" in our partnership
>            agreement.  And I can't really say I'm torn
>            up about Ben's early demise.

>                    AMOS
>            A motive, Miss Lee.  An Oldie, but a Goodie.
>            Greed.  The double-handed variety.

>                              (CONTINUED)

28   CONTINUED: - 2

KeeKee snaps her finger at one of her ASSISTANT girls, a
cutie-pie, and the girl brings her a long brass telescope.
KeeKee takes it and starts to turn toward the Photographer
and her set-up.  She pauses.

                    KEEKEE
          Speaking of motives, as long as we're
          clocking the murder sweepstakes, what
          odds do you give on hate?

                    AMOS
          It's a fast runner-up.

                    KEEKEE
          Then put on your track shoes, Captain,
          because my double-handed greed is going
          to look awfully puny next to some other
          people's hate.

                    AMOS
          Benjamin Glory had enemies.

                    KEEKEE
          Why not, he was an ogre.  A louse.  A
          two-timing, philandering, crooked cockroach
          with the personality of a king cobra.  He
          was...

                              SHARP CUT TO:

29   ANGLE PAST ANJANETTE & SABLE TO TIM
               talks
     as he ~~walks up~~ to them.  Anjanette speaks with an accent.

                    ANJANETTE
          ...a ~~xxxxxxxxxxxx~~ sweet, kind man with
          love for everyone; a fine person, a man
          of honor, and a brilliant businessman.
          He has saved Glory Lee Frocks time and
          again from the mistakes of KeeKee.

                    SABLE
               (wryly)
          He was Big Daddy to everyone.  A doll.

                    TIM
          That's fine, ladies, but he must have been
          on someone's hate list.

                              (CONTINUED)

29    CONTINUED:

                         ANJANETTE
          Why do you say that?

                         TIM
          Because the morgue squad had to use
          blotters to get him off the floor
          of that elevator.

     Both women's faces register shock.

                         ANJANETTE
          Oh!  That is terrible, just terrible.

                         SABLE
                         (furious)
          You see, Mother!  I told you!  I told
          you!  Your possessiveness has done it
          again...oh, I hate you!

                         ANJANETTE
          Shut up, just be quiet!  What do you know!

     Sable, in tears, spins suddenly, and runs away.  Tim and
     Anjanette stare after her.

                         TIM
          She seemed upset about Glory's death.
          Were they good friends?

                         ANJANETTE
                         (sharply)
          Everyone was friends with Benjamin.  He
          was a fine man.  Sable is very high-strung.
                         (beat)
          This will mean an altering of my designs.

                         TIM
          Why is that?

                         ANJANETTE
                         (points across room)
          That woman.  Le cochon!  The pig.  KeeKee
          Lee.  If there is one for whom Benjamin's
          death is advantageous, it is she.

                         TIM
          Because she now owns the line alone?

                         ANJANETTE
          Exactly.  She is a reptile, she would
          kill for a dollar, she has no talent, no
          design sense, no intuition about high...

                              SHARP CUT TO:

30      SAME AS 28

KeeKee looks through the telescope at the model being
photographed.  She speaks to Amos.

                    KEEKEE
        ...fashion is big business.  We dictate
        what women will wear and how they think,
        and even what kind of morality their
        clothes call for.
                    (to Photographer)
        Hey!  Eagle-Eye!  Slit that number down the
        back and stuff it with tissue paper.  I want
        a fuller look!

Eagle-Eye starts to move toward the model.  From her
jeans she whips out a straight-razor.

31      ANJANETTE & TIM

as she reaches behind a drapery and pulls out a megaphone.
She howls at Eagle-Eye.

                    ANJANETTE
        Leave it alone, Eagle-Eye!  It is a natural
        line...if you puff it we cheat the customer.

32      KEEKEE & AMOS

KeeKee with the telescope, bellows at Eagle-Eye.

                    KEEKEE
        Slit it, Eagle-Eye.  That old crone
        doesn't know what'll sell!

Across the room they shriek at each other.

                    ANJANETTE
        Leave it as it is.  That...that murderess
        has the taste of a petit bourgeois dolt.
        I won't let her add thievery to her other
        crimes.

                    KEEKEE
        Cut it up, Eagle-Eye.  That nitwit is so
        busy keeping her trampy daughter off the
        streets she can't keep up with fashion.
        And if she calls me one more name I'll
        stuff this telescope down her idiot throat!

Eagle-Eye stops, starts, stops, starts.  Finally throws
up her hands.
                    PHOTOGRAPHER
        Okay, Penny, move out.  Send me Francine.

The model leaves, another comes in, assumes position.

33    MEDIUM SHOT   AMOS & KEEKEE

Amos pulls her around.   She is boiling mad at Anajnette.

> AMOS
> Take it easy.  This is more important
> than any petty brawls.

> KEEKEE
> Listen, Captain, I have a quarter million
> dollar a year operation here.  There are
> only three kinds of dress manufacturers
> in this city.  One is a mass produce house
> that makes medium-priced garments, the
> second is a "knock-off" house that does
> the same thing for peanuts and sells out
> of chain stores, and there's Glory Lee.
> (beat)
> I'm all alone.  I'm a coutouriere.  That
> means the High Lama of fashion.  I can't
> ignore any details.  So no brawl is a
> minor brawl.

She half-turns and yells over her shoulder.

> KEEKEE
> Color blind!

Anjanette screams back.

> ANJANETTE'S VOICE O.S.
> Clown!  Tasteless!  Hausfrau!

> AMOS
> I'd suggest you stop yelling for a moment,
> Miss Lee.  Or you're liable to find yourself
> wearing some high fashion stripes.  In a
> cell downtown.

> KEEKEE
> I didn't kill Ben.  If you want a prime
> suspect, try his wife Carlene.  She was
> getting fed to the teeth with his
> playing hanky and/or panky with my models.

> AMOS
> You used the plural.

> KEEKEE
> So did Ben.

(CONTINUED)

33   CONTINUED:

                    AMOS
          I'll need a list of names.

                    KEEKEE
          Why bother.  Anything in skirts you
          see around here had its bottom pinched
          by Ben.  Everyone but Mrs. Machree--and
          the only reason he left <u>her</u> alone was
          she threatened him with a steam iron.

                    AMOS
          And you?  Is your name on that list?

                    KEEKEE
          Not a chance.  With me, business is
          business.

                    AMOS
          What about your designer over there,
          what's her name...?

                    KEEKEE
          Anjanette Delacroix.  Chances are
          good, though I don't know for sure.

                    AMOS
          And the daughter?  Her name is...

                                   SHARP CUT TO:

34   MEDIUM SHOT   ANJANETTE & TIM

                    ANJANETTE
          Sable.  I was with her last night,
          and we came to work together this
          morning.

                    TIM
          We'll have to check that, you know.

                    ANJANETTE
          Check, check.  Check all you like.  I
          had no reason to kill Benjamin Glory.
          I came from Switzerland ten years ago
          to design for him.  He gave me all the
          Help and encouragement...

                    TIM
          You're Swiss?  But you have a French
          accent.

                                   (CONTINUED)

34    CONTINUED:

                         ANJANETTE
          Many Swiss do, Detective.  I am from
          St. Gallen, near Lake Zurich; there
          are many French there.  Most Swiss
          speak with a French accent, as a matter
          of fact.

Tim looks at her curiously, but no comment is made.

                         TIM
          I'd like to look through the shop, if
          you have the time to show me...

At that moment Anjanette pulls out her megaphone again,
and begins screaming at Eagle-Eye, the photographer.

                         ANJANETTE
          Use clothes pins at the back of the
          skirt, pull it tight, much tighter!

KeeKee begins screaming across the room, with her telescope
at her eye.

                         KEEKEE
          Leave it full, it looks skimpy!

                         ANJANETTE
          Eagle-Eye, ignore that fool, do as I
          say!

                         KEEKEE
          Go ahead, Eagle-Eye, and if Methusaleh
          doesn't like it, she can resign!

                         ANJANETTE
          I own stock, don't forget that, you
          murdereress!  I know you killed our
          poor Benjamin!

                         KEEKEE
          That does it!  I've had it with you,
          Miss Crowbait of '64!

They charge toward the model, both of them.  Anjanette
starts to pull the dress tight, KeeKee tries to loosen
it, and the beautiful model is dragged around the
podium.  As they fight, Amos and Tim come together
again beside Eagle-Eye, the photogrpaher.

35   3-SHOT   AMOS, TIM & PHOTOGRAPHER

as they watch the two women struggling, pulling and fighting
over the model.  Tim and Amos talk across Eagle-Eye as though
they were watching a flower show, quietly, unhurriedly.

> AMOS
> Learn anything?

> TIM
> Anjanette Delacroix and her daughter
> don't get along.  She says she was
> with her all night and this morning.

> AMOS
> You'll have to check the daughter out.

> TIM
> No problem.  You find out anything?

> AMOS
> Glory played around a lot.  But the
> Lee woman thinks his wife did it.

> TIM
> That's interesting.  Show her the
> eagle insignia?

> AMOS
> No.  We'll probably have to come back.
> (to Eagle-Eye)
> You don't get much work done between
> those two, do you?

> PHOTOGRAPHER
> Does an aardvark adore apricots?

At that moment KeeKee and Anjanette pull at the model so
furiously, the dress rips off her completely, revealing
the girl standing in the briefest possible attire.

Tim and Amos turn away, shocked and at a loss.

> AMOS
> (to Eagle-Eye)
> Tell 'em not to leave town.  We'll
> be back.

Tim and Amos stumble away, shattered.

> FADE OUT.

## ACT II

FADE IN:

36    EXT. GLORY MANSION   (ESTABLISHING  DAY (STOCK)

The Rolls parked outside the house.

37    INT. GLORY MANSION  DAY

as EXT. CLOSEUP of BLACK FRAME becomes the rear end of a
hunched-over man rushing toward CARLENE GLORY, who is dressed
in a sexy imitation of a matador's costume. The man is the
butler, GRIPPSHOLM and he wears a set of bull's horns. They
are conducting a <u>corrida</u> in the sumptuous living room, with
Carlene Glory using her cape and shouting Ole's as the poor
old butler (at least sixty years old) goes staggering past.

Carlene Glory is a looker. An ex-showgirl with much pazzaz.

As Amos enters, Grippsholm goes shooting past, Carlene
executes a perfect <u>veronica</u> and the butler smashes full into th
the wall. He sags down with a silly look on his face, the
horns hanging slantwise. A vase tumbles off a table, smashes.

>               CARLENE
>              (annoyed)
> Oh, Grippsholm, you clumsy, you!  Now
> see what you've done. That was a Tang
> Dynasty vase. You're a better butler
> than a bull, that's for sure.

>               AMOS
> Mrs. Glory?

>               CARLENE
>              (turning)
> Ole!

>               AMOS
> Gesundheit.

>               CARLENE
> I didn't hear you come in; did you
> ring?

>               AMOS
> I let myself in. No butler.

>              . CARLENE
>              (looks at butler)
> You're right. No butler. Ole!

38     ANOTHER ANGLE   ON CARLENE

as she swirls cape onto sofa and goes to portable bar for a
pitcher of water.  She takes it to Grippsholm and begins
pouring it on him to revive him.

                    CARLENE
          How will I ever stay in trim if poor
          old Grippsholm doesn't stay on his feet?

                    AMOS
          You're a matador?

                    CARLENE
          Just a hobby.  Everyone needs a healthy
          hobby.  I used to be a dancer, chorus
          line, you know; this is the best way to
          keep my figure.
                    (beat)
          Eh, toro!  Welcome back!

Grippsholm stumbles to his feet, glazed-eyed, and marks a
weaving path out of the room.  Carlene calls after him.

                    CARLENE
                    (continues)
          Go lie down, Grippsholm, I'll call
          you later.

She turns back to Amos, pitcher of water still in hands.

                    AMOS
          I'm Captain Amos Burke...

                    CARLENE
          Care for a drink?

                    AMOS
          No thanks, I, uh, have some bad news
          for you.  It's about your husband...

                    CARLENE
          I don't want to hear it.

                    AMOS
          But...

                    CARLENE
                    (mixing drink at
                     bar)
          Nope, not a bit of it.  I'm fed up with
          Benny and his shenanigans.  Ever since
          he came back from the war...

                              (CONTINUED)

38    CONTINUED:

                         AMOS
     The war?

                         CARLENE
     Yes, of course.  World War Two.  You
     must have heard about it...it was in
     all the papers.

                         AMOS
     Oh, yes, now I recall a vicious rumor
     about some trouble over there.

                         CARLENE
     Certainly, that's the one.  Well, ever
     since Benny came back in forty-five,
     he's just been a monster.  He was such
     a good husband, but you know, I think
     war does something to people...it sort
     of brutalizes them.

                         AMOS
     War is hell.

                         CARLENE
     You can say that again...no, don't bother.
     Well, what I mean is, Benny started having
     one affair after another with the models
     at the shop...
                         (beat)
     ...he owns half of Glory Lee Frocks, you
     know.

                         AMOS
     Mrs. Glory, perhaps you'd better listen
     to what I have to say about your husband...

                         CARLENE
     No, I just do not want to hear it.  If
     you're someone's husband, that's your
     problem.  As for Benny, this new girl is
     k just one too many.  Setting her up
     in her own apartment, well!  I tell you
     I'm through, all done, I'm going to
     divorce him...

                         AMOS
     You don't have to bother.

                              8        (CONTINUED)

38    CONTINUED: - 2

                    CARLENE
          Oh, yes I do, too.  Half of the community
          property comes to, uh, let's see...

She goes to a desk, starts to figure it out.

39    CLOSEUP    AMOS

as he walks up behind her.

                    AMOS
          Your husband is dead, Mrs. Glory.
          He was killed in an elevator crash
          at the Ellison Building this morning.
          He was murdered.

She drops the pencil.

                    CARLENE
          Who did you say you were?

                    AMOS
          Captain Burke, from Homicide.  I'm sorry
          to have broken the news in that way, but...

                    CARLENE
                    (indignant)
          Well, I think that's just a stinky
          thing for Benny to do.  Why I was going
          to really make him sweat.

                    AMOS
          You say he had a new girl friend?

                    CARLENE
          Why, that ratfink, getting bumped off
          like that.  What a nerve!  I had all
          sorts of trouble planned, as soon as I
          found out who this new flame was.

                    AMOS
          You didn't know her name?

                    CARLENE
          What a chicken, what an absolute chicken.
          To take the easy way out.  And him a
          Colonel in the US Army, which he was so
          proud of, and his war experiences.  Why,
          that's simply cowardice in the face of
          a divorce.  I think I'd better call my
          attorney.

40   ANOTHER ANGLE

as Amos pulls the Colonel's insignia from his pocket.

>                    AMOS
>          You say he was a Colonel in the
>          US Army?

>                    CARLENE
>          Oh, all over Europe after the Occupation.
>          Why that miserable, conniving...
>                    (beat)
>          I'll bet he committed suicide, that's what!

>                    AMOS
>          No, he was murdered.  Where were you, by the
>          way, at nine o'clock this morning?

>                    CARLENE
>          In bed asleep, where everyone should be at
>          that ghastly hour.  Where were you?

>                    AMOS
>          Any witnesses?

>                    CARLENE
>          I **beg** your pardon!  I'm a married woman.

>                    AMOS
>          No offense, Mrs. Glory.  I just meant,
>          did any servants see you, perhaps?

>                    CARLENE
>          My maid, Grippsholm the butler, my
>          pedicurist, my hairdresser, the housekeeper
>          and my sleepteacher.

>                    AMOS
>          All of them?  While you were in bed?

>                    CARLENE
>          I sleep very soundly.  I'm learning
>          Italian in my sleep.

Grippsholm returns.  She takes up her cape, and they start
parrying each other.

>                    AMOS
>          So you were going to divorce him.

>                    CARLENE
>          It wouldn't have worked.  Benny never would
>          have let me go.  It was safer having affairs
>          with those models while he was attached.
>          But I'd have given it a try.

41    ANGLE ON AMOS  PAST CARLENE & BUTLER

                    AMOS
          You don't seem too unhappy about
          his death.

                    CARLENE
                  (stops parrying)
          Upset?  I'm de-stroyed!  How can I keep
          in shape with Benny gone?  He's been
          having such aggravation about those
          stolen dress designs, I could have
          worked simply pounds off chasing him
          around late at night, bugging him
          when he couldn't sleep.  Like last
          night...

                    AMOS
          Last night?

                    CARLENE
          About 4:30, he received a phone call.
          Something about the theft and re-sale
          of fashion secrets.  Why, he was just
          livid.  It was a wonderful hour before
          he left.  I chased him all over the
          place annoying him.
                  (beat)
          I must have lost a good quarter-inch
          off my hips.

                    AMOS
          He got a call at 4:30 and left the
          house?

                    CARLENE
          Why, yes.

                    AMOS
          Who called?

                    CARLENE
          How should I know?  I only heard a
          little bit of it as I woke up.  But
          I'll bet if Benny hadn't been killed,
          I'd have had some great reducing
          sessions...this would have ruined his
          sleep for weeks.

     Amos starts toward door as Carlene resumes her bullfighting.

                    AMOS
          I'll be back in touch with you, Mrs.
          Glory.  If you remember anything, you
          can reach me through my office downtown.

42    CLOSEUP    CARLENE

with Grippsholm maneuving behind her, she turns to Amos.

                    CARLENE
          If anything comes up, I'll cal, you.
          And if you're free later, come on back, we
          can work out in the gym...

At that moment Grippsholm charges, and knocks her sprawling.

                    CARLENE
                   (continues)
          Ole, Grippsholm, you old coot, Ole!
          I knew there was life in that carcass of
          yours.

She bounds to her feet and they go at it hot and heavy with
Grippsholm really trying to clobber her, as Amos leaves.

                                    DISSOLVE TO:

43    EXT. SABLE'S BUILDING  ESTABLISHING  DAY

a LONG SHOT that TRAVELS UP the face of the building and
ZOOMS IN on the penthouse.

44    INT. SABLE'S HALLWAY  DAY

as Tim, consulting notebook, comes down hall.  He looks at
one door after another, finally selects one, pushes doorbell.
Hold for several beats, and then the door opens quickly,
and a HAND PULLS HIM IN by the collar.  He does a Mack
Sennett flip through the doorway.

45    INT. SABLE'S APARTMENT  ESTABLISHING  DAY

Sable, in a bikini, has yanked Tim through the door.  The
apartment is beautiful, very modern, very light, and overlooks
the city.

                    TIM
          Miss, uh, Delacroix, I'm uh...

                    SABLE
          Yes, I remember you from the showroom.
                   (½ beat)
          Do you think I'm lovely?

                    TIM
                   (embarassed)
          Why, yes, I think you're just fine.

                                    (CONTINUED)

45    CONTINUED:

                              SABLE
                           (pouting)
              Is that all: just fine?

                              TIM
              Why, no...I uh think you're beautiful.

Sable considers him a moment.  Then walks to a bookcase,
takes out a book, hands it to him.

                              SABLE
              You won't do at all.  Now look under
              BEAUTY COMMA WOMEN and come up with
              some good lines.

                              TIM
                           (looks at book)
              "Great Quotations & AphorismsM For
              All Occasions"?

                              SABLE
              Right.  I'm too beautiful for you to
              just address me like any other girl,
              so while I slip into something more
              comfortable, you figure out some better
              words...

She moves toward bedroom.

                              TIM
                           (stunned)
              More comfortable?

But she is gone.  Tim looks around for a while, here and
there, and then starts toward the bedroom.  He spies
another bedroom door, and tries it.  Open.  He enters
the room.

46    INT. BEDROOM  DAY

as Tim looks around.  He opens drawers, generally snoops.
He tries the closet, and opening it wide, sees a number
of men's suits and...a US Army uniform.  A Colonel's
uniform.  He examines it so CAMERA CLOSEUP on Colonel's
insignia is obvious.  Both of them are on lapels.  He also
sees a bath robe with the initials B.G. on the front.

He closes the closet door and returns to the living room
with the book.  He shuffles through, picking the section she
indicated.

47     ANGLE PAST TIM

to bedroom doorway as Sable opens door.  The SOUND of a huge
gong being struck.  Sable emerges in high heels and filmy
negligee, holding a hand-mirror, looking at herself.  Tim
now realizes the entire apartment is <u>filled</u> with mirrors, and
one entire wall is made up of segmented mirrors.

> SABLE
> Someone gave me a dinner gong as a
> birthday present.  I like to make
> a big entrance.  Oooo, whatta doll I am!

Tim hurriedly consults the book of aphorisms.

> TIM
> (quoting)
> "She walks in beauty, like the night
> Of cloudless climes and starry skies..."
> Lord Byron, 1788 to 1824.

> SABLE
> Not bad for openers, not bad at all.
> You're learning.

> TIM
> I'd like to learn a lot more.

Sable slinks to a mirror, examines herself.

> SABLE
> That could be taken as a sexy remark,
> Detective Tillman.

> TIM
> Tilson.  It could, but that wasn't
> really what I had in mind.

> SABLE
> (suddenly)
> What do you mean by that, huh, what do
> you mean by that?  Aren't I lovely,
> desireable, compelling, maddening?

> TIM
> Every guy's dream of romance.

> SABLE
> Not flowery enough.

Tim leafs through book, selects another one he has marked
by a finger.

48    2-SHOT   TIM & SABLE

from Tim in B.G. to Sable, examining her teeth in a mirror.

                    TIM
                 (quoting)
        "Kindness in women, not their
        beauteous looks, Shall win my
        love."  Shakespeare, "The Taming
        Of The Shrew."


                    SABLE
        You're trying to tell me something.


                    TIM
        Mmm-hmmm.  Now it's your turn.


                    SABLE
                 (pirouetting)
        What would you like me to tell you?
        I know all kindsa stuff.


                    TIM
        Try starting with Benjamin Glory.


                    SABLE
        You pick some peculiar starting places.


                    TIM
        You pick some peculiar bathrobes.

A quizzical expression changes to one of resigned understanding
as Sable glances toward the other bedroom door.

                    SABLE
        Oh-ho, so that's how you want it. Down
        and dirty.


                    TIM
        Was it?


                    SABLE
        That calls for a slap in the chops, young
        cop.


                    TIM
        "A woman who strikes a man is not a lady."


                    SABLE
        Who said that?


                    TIM
        Amos Burke.  One of his laws.

49    REVERSE ANGLE

REFLECTION of SABLE IN MIRROR with TIM IN B.G. as she
primps and studies herself.

                    SABLE
          You're trying to find something nasty
          where there isn't anything of the kind.
          Mr. Glory was a friend, that's all. We
          had a strictly platonic relationship.

                    TIM
          He just found it convenient to come here
          to take his showers.

                    SABLE
          You've got a one-track gutter.

                    TIM
          It's like the joke about the guy who goes
          to the psychiatrist...you're the one who's
          showing the naughty pictures.

                    SABLE
          Okay, so sue me. He had eyes for me, and
          he set me up here. So what? So I'm a
          tax deduction. That was as far as it
          went.

                    TIM
          There's a vicious rumor he was leaving his
          wife for another girl. You fit the word.

                    SABLE
          Fat chance. In this state, he'd have lost
          half of everything. Ben was a swinger,
          but he wasn't stupid.

                    TIM
          So he just kept his clothes here for, uh,
          emergencies.

                    SABLE
          Listen, stop banging on that note, will you.
          He liked to get away from his wife's nagging
          --she's the World's Foremost Annoyance
          Machine, a walking mental ward--and he came
          here for a lot of silence.

                    TIM
          What about the Colonel's uniform?

                              (CONTINUED)

49    CONTINUED:

As Sable swings away from the mirror, relying now on the
hand-glass she carries.

                    SABLE
        He was a goof for the Army.  He did a
        big tour overseas during World War Two,
        and stayed in the Reserves.  He kept
        the uniform here for meeting nights.

                    TIM
        But there wasn't anything between you
        two.

                    SABLE
        There might have been, I won't deny
        that, but he didn't really have the
        time.  I've only been living here
        about two weeks now.

                    TIM
        I can check that out with the manager...

                    SABLE
        You should live and be well, buhbee;
        check and double-check.  You'll find out
        I'm telling the truth.

                    TIM
        And that's what you and your mother were
        hasseling this afternoon?

                    SABLE
        True.  She thought my having moved out
        on her, my living here, made me look bad.
        But she's so possessive anyhow, it seems
        the lesser of two evils.

                    TIM
        What about Glory and the other models?

                    SABLE
                  (shrugging)
        I've heard about it.  So what?  He was
        a decent-enough guy.  He treated me
        right, and if he intended to start playing
        kissy-face, at least he had the sense to
        wait.  I never had to duck and dodge.

                    TIM
        I'm almost inclined to believe you.

50    ANOTHER ANGLE

> SABLE
> Will miracles never cease.
>
> TIM
> One more thing: I understand you and your
> mother are of Swiss extraction.
>
> SABLE
> That's right.  I was born over there.  We
> came to America about ten years ago so
> Mother could work for Glory Lee.
>
> TIM
> And how long have you been modelling for the
> firm?
>
> SABLE
> About eight months.  Since I turned
> nineteen.  But I've been gorgeous for
> quite a while now.
>
> TIM
> You're a princess, no doubt about it.
>
> SABLE
> I hope that isn't your parting shot.

Tim leafs through the book again, selects a quote:

> TIM
> "He who is in love with himself has at
> least this advantage--he won't encounter
> many rivals for in his love."  Lichtenberg.

He tosses the book on the sofa, and whistling smugly,
heads for the door.  He opens door just as the hand-
mirror shatters beside his head.  Around the open door
Tim grins back at her.

> TIM
> (continues)
> At the speed you're going, lady, that
> ought to net you about <u>eight</u> years
> bad luck.

He slams door.  CAMERA HOLDS a beat on Sable, who slowly
looks back over her shoulder at the mirror--with a
concerned expression.  She runs her hand softly over her
face...as though she had found terrifying lines suddenly.
SPECIAL EFFECT: <u>lines</u> <u>appear</u> and a frightened look lives
on her face.

> DISSOLVE THRU TO:

51    INT. POLICE LAB  ESTABLISHING    DAY

EXT. CLOSEUP on a very small puppy dog (<u>NOT</u>, repeat, <u>NOT</u>
a poodle, just some kinda muttpup) sitting on a desk, amid
stacks of papers.  A hand enters frame and spoon-feeds him
something puppy-delicious.  CAMERA PULLS BACK to reveal
McCloud, sitting at his desk, veterinarianing to the dog.
Amos and Tim stand over him, looking bemused, grinning.

                    McCLOUD
                    (piqued)
          Nobody's perfect.

                    AMOS
          You're a foul ball, George.

                    McCLOUD
          Well, he <u>looked</u> as though he'd died in
          the elevator crash...

                    TIM
          I remember he said he was positive, Captain.

                    AMOS
          I recall the same thing, Tim.

                    TIM
          Or he'd go back to being a vet, isn't
          that what he said, sir?

                    AMOS
          Precisely, as I recall, Tim.  Precisely.

                    McCLOUD
                    (surly)
          Get off my back.

                    AMOS
          Frightening how inept some of our civil
          servants have become, isn't it, Detective
          Tilson?

                    TIM
          A cause for civic concern, Captain.

                    AMOS
          Do they still guillotine people, Detective?

                    TIM
          I think this state favors bamboo shoots under
          the fingernails.

                              (CONTINUED)

51    CONTINUED:

McCloud pulls a report out from under the pup.

> McCLOUD
> One more remark out of you clowns and
> I'll eat my words. Literally. And you
> can go whistle for this supplementary.

> AMOS
> All right, George, take it easy. Anyone
> can make a mistake...

> McCLOUD
> (mollified)
> Well, I'm glad you recognize that...

> AMOS
> ...and yours was leaving the dog and cat
> hospital.

> McCLOUD
> Okay! That does it! Out! Out!

Tim and Amos break up at McCloud's annoyance. They calm him
down to a semblance of sanity.

> TIM
> All right, George, okay, just take it
> easy. What does the supplementary say?

> McCLOUD
> (reluctantly)
> Well, if you hadn't badgered me, we probably
> wouldn't have come across what we did. I was
> so set on getting it pinned down exactly this
> time, that we went over Glory with everything
> but a clam rake.

> AMOS
> Ah, the wonders of forensic medicine.

> McCLOUD
> Why are you haunting me?
> (beat)
> He died from a fractured skull, all right,
> but not in that elevator crash. He was
> struck repeatedly with a sharp and blunt
> instrument.

(CONTINUED)

51     CONTINUED: - 2

> TIM
> (startledly)
> Sharp _and_ blunt?  Is that possible?
> What kind of weapon fits _that_ description?

> McCLOUD
> (grinning like shark)
> That's _your_ problem.
> (beat)
> But here's a minor fact that may help you.
> In cleaning out the wound, among the bits
> of bone and matted hair we found traces of
> an organic compound found in plant-cells,
> a member of the amylose group of carbohydrates.

> AMOS
> Pardon?

> McCLOUD
> (relishing)
> A substance obtained by interlarding unequal
> parts flour and water, commonly referred to
> by chemists as $(C_6H_{10}O_5)x$.

> AMOS
> Pardon?

> McCLOUD
> (grinning)
> Common ironing starch.

They stare at him a beat, then turn to leave.  Amos opens
door and throws punchline:

> AMOS
> Don't fret, George.  If you can't make it
> as a vet, I have friends in the sanitation
> department...

George blows.  He snaps at the itty-bitty puppy:

> McCLOUD
> (viciously)
> Fang!  Kill!  Kill, Fang!

The puppy flops over and plays dead.  McCloud is destroyed.
Amos and Tim laugh, leave the room.

52    INT. HALLWAY  HOMICIDE DIVISION  DAY

as they emerge from the Lab, Les comes limping down the hall,
shoes in hand. He looks weary. His tie is undone, his hat
is back on his head. They pause and wait for him.

                    AMOS
          Well, if it isn't the wandering minstrel.

                    LES
          I covered that fifth floor like a sticking
          plaster. I must have walked fifty miles.

                    TIM
          How's your mad killer theory working out?

                    LES
          Couldn't find a thing. But I know Glory
          wasn't the target...there's nothing on that
          fifth floor that has anything to do with
          Glory Lee except a storage room where they
          keep those dress models.

                    AMOS
          Well?

                    LES
          So the killer still had no way of knowing
          the car would contain only Glory and dummies.

Amos walks toward office. They follow. Amos opens door.

                    AMOS
          Inside. Let's play all this back.

They follow him in.

53    INT. AMOS' OFFICE  ESTABLISHING  DAY

as they enter. Amos behind desk, Tim draped over bookcase,
Les collapsed in chair, massaging feet.

                    AMOS
          Carlene Glory made reference to stolen
          fashion secrets. Glory got a call early
          this morning, and went to the building,
          to follow up on the theft. Either one
          of you get anything on that angle?

They both shake heads negative. Amos looks disturbed.

                              (CONTINUED)

53   CONTINUED:

                              AMOS
          KeeKee Lee had a motive.  Power grab for
          Glory's half of the operation.  Nothing
          on either Sable or Anjanette Delacroix:
          both had to lose if Glory died.  And we
          come up empty on anyone else eligible.

                              TIM
          What about this selling secrets business?

                              AMOS
          Our only point of reference is Carlene Glory
          on that aspect.

                              LES
          So what about the widow?  I've heard of it
          before.

                              AMOS
          Possible.  But I doubt it.  She's not really
          the world's brightest woman, and if it was
          her, she's got a tough alibi to crack.

                              LES
          Well, I have this theory...

                              TIM
          Les, I hate to break it to you, but Glory
          wasn't killed in the crash.  His head was
          beaten in before he was tossed into that
          car.  They found starch in the skull wound.

Les throws up his hands.  He is discouraged.

                              LES
          Okay, Glory was the target.  Maybe I'm just
          getting old.

                              AMOS
          It was a grand idea, and it might have
          worked, if McCloud hadn't come up with
          a supplementary.

                              LES
          So which way now, Gallant Captain?

                              AMOS
          Starch.  Hmmm.  Let's go back to the Glory
          Lee plant.

They rise and leave.

                              DISSOLVE THRU:

54   RUNNING SHOT   STREET   (STOCK)   DAY

as Rolls passes through.

DISSOLVE THRU TO:

55   EXT. ELLISON BUILDING   ESTABLISHING   DAY

with Rolls parked out front, Henry polishing windshield.

DISSOLVE THRU TO:

56   INT. GLORY LEE WORKROOM   ESTABLISHING   DAY

a long room with half a dozen ~~xxxxxxxxxx~~ sewing machines
in rows, tended by extremely pretty young girls. Behind
them, four steam ironing boards. Off to one side a long
waist-high counter with bundles of fabric being separated
by three other girls. (NOTE: for exact set-up of this
scene, author suggests contacting Larry Chrysler or Eve
Le Coq of Eve Le Coq Fashions--MA. 7-5673 who will allow
a visit to their workrooms. This detail is strongly recommended.)
One of the steam ironing women is not young. It is Mrs.
Machree. She is the only older woman present.

> KEEKEE'S VOICE O.S.
> This is the "factory". Most firms have
> much bigger operations, but since we
> deal only in couturiere fashions, we
> need less help.

A rack of garments is wheeled past by a young girl. As it
passes CAMERA TRACKS BACK and we see Amos and Les with
KeeKee. They walk through the operation.

> KEEKEE
> These are the sewers. The ironers are called
> "operators". Over there those girls are
> called "bundlers".

> LES
> These girls seem much younger and prettier
> than I'd expected them to be.

> KEEKEE
> One of Ben's little peculiarities. Most
> factories use older women, but Ben liked to
> look at pretty faces, so...

> AMOS
> I see Mrs. Machree over there. How did
> she slip in?

> KEEKEE
> She's the Floor Lady, been here since we
> started in business. Ben was fond of her.

57    INTERCUT   MRS. MACHREE

as she works over her steam iron board.

                    AMOS' VOICE O.S.
                    (very interested)
         Oh, really...hmmm...

58    ANOTHER SHOT   AMOS, LES & KEEKEE

as Amos takes a step toward Mrs. Machree, there is the sound
of SHOUTING from behind them, and they turn to see Tim being
pushed out of a small side room with glass windows.  Anjanette
Delacroix pushes him out.

                    ANJANETTE
         Spy!   Thief!   Out!   Out!

Amos turns to KeeKee for explanation.

                    KEEKEE
         That's the design room.  Anjanette is a
         nut about it.  She'd have armed guards
         if we let her.

                    AMOS
         Perhaps she had good cause.

                    KEEKEE
         What is that supposed to mean?

                    AMOS
         Carlene Glory says someone was boosting
         your designs.

KeeKee looks startled that Amos knows this.

                    KEEKEE
         How did she find out?  I thought only
         Benjamin and myself knew about it...
         both of us, and the thief.

                    AMOS
         She knows.  And I know.  Is it true?

                    KEEKEE
         Yes.  But the designs haven't turned up
         yet.  Whoever got them out of here--and
         I don't know how they did it--must have
         sold them to a knock-off house.

Tim comes up to them.

                    TIM
         She won't let me in there, Captain.

59     ANOTHER ANGLE   ON AMOS

                              AMOS
                    Wait a second, Tim.
                             (to KeeKee)
                    What's a "knock-off house"?

                              KEEKEE
                    A _schlock_ outfit.  If we buy fifty yards of
                    fabric and make a number and do well with
                    it, they'll buy. xxkkxxxxxxxd twenty thousand
                    yards, cut corners on the construction, mass
                    produce it, and get it into the shops at
                    a fraction of what our original costs.

                              AMOS
                    Doesn't seem as though that could hurt you.

                              KEEKEE
                    No, not if it's six months later, after we're
                    peaking our sales.  But if they get the design
                    before we ship, then they take up that six
                    month lag, and we're clobbered.

                              AMOS
                    And that's what has been happening.

                              KEEKEE
                    Right.  And now Ben's been killed, just when
                    he was hot on the trail of who sold us out.

                              AMOS
                    Well, I wouldn't worry about it.  I think
                    I've found your spy.

                              KEEKEE
                    Who?

                              AMOS
                    The killer of Benjamin Glory.

                              TIM
                    You know who the killer is, Captain?

                              AMOS
                    You can help me make the arrest.

He starts walking down the line, toward the steam iron
boards.  He pauses before Mrs. Machree.

                              AMOS
                             (continues)
                    Les, the cuffs.

Les hands him the cuffs while Mrs. Machree and others
stare at him in disbelief.

60     CLOSEUP   AMOS & MRS. MACHREE

as he slips the cuffs on her.

                    AMOS
        I arrest you for the murder of Benjamin
        Glory, and warn you that anything you
        say may be used against you.

                  MRS. MACHREE
        You're putting me on!

                    TIM
        Captain, are you sure?

                    AMOS
        Positive, Tim. Look at the beady little
        eyes, the ruthless mouth, the sinister
        shadows in her face. This is a killer,
        Tim, a vicious rotten killer. Take her
        away.

Tim, bewilderedly, grasps the other cuff and starts to
pull kindly-looking old Mrs. Machree away.

                    AMOS
        And take this with you. Don't smudge it.

He unplugs the steam iron and hands it to Tim. Tim starts
away with the old lady. She stops and starts yelling.

                  MRS. MACHREE
              (incongruously)
        You'll never take me alive, copper! No
        cage can hold me, you'll see, I'll bust out!
        I'll get you, fuzz, you'll see!

Tim drags her away, screaming violently. Amos turns to
confront KeeKee and Les's amazed stares.

                    AMOS
              (shrugging)
      Hm! Who'd have thought it?

He walks away, whistling, toward the design room, as KeeKee,
Les and the entire roomful of girls stares after him.

                         FADE OUT.

ACT III


FADE IN:

61   INT. DESIGN ROOM   ESTABLISHING   DAY

MED. CLOSEUP on a huge ½ round cardboard container with the
words        CALL FERGIE FOR PICK-UP OF YOUR RAGS
                    MA. 7-9954

on it. The barrel is stuffed with old bits and pieces of
cloth. CAMERA PANS AWAY from the barrel, across a long
(10 yds x 45" wide) Masonite-covered cutting table, about
38" high. A man stands at the table cutting samples from
forms. Across the room is a series of metal racks containing
bolts and sample cuts of hundreds of different fabrics. A
young girl sits at another steam ironer in a corner. Overhead
flourescents light the room. Dress designs hang on the
walls. A dress dummy has a fling of cloth thrown across
one shoulder. At a table identical to the cutting table,
on the other side of the room, an ASSISTANT DESIGNER is
laying the "samples" cut by the man on sheets of brown paper,
and moving them around to fit them properly on the sheet,
then marking their shapes with thick pencil marks. CAMERA
PULLS BACK as Anjanette comes into frame and pulls the younger
girl away from the marker sheet. She is furious.

                         ANJANETTE
              Clumsy! Epileptic! Your marker's not
              tight enough, re-lay it, you're wasting
              yardage! You want to cost us a fortune?

Amos moves in behind her.

                         AMOS
              It looks tight to me.

                         ANJANETTE
              I once knew an Assistant Designer who
              made thirty thousand dollars by laying a
              pattern on the bias, losing yardage so
              the company had to buy more than it really
              needed, and wound up in prison. I'm the
              Designer here, Captain, so kindly be still.

                         AMOS
              You seem extraordinarily nervous, Mrs.
              Delacroix.

                         ANJANETTE
              Who wouldn't be, with the terrible things
              that have happened here today.

62    2-SHOT  AMOS & ANJANETTE

as she picks up her megaphone from a chair, goes to the door
of the design room, opens it and yells out:

>           ANJANETTE
>           (yelling)
>       Send in the meat!

She closes the door and turns back to Amos.

>           AMOS
>       Well, now that we've caught the killer, there
>       should be no need for you to be upset.

>           ANJANETTE
>       That poor, poor Mrs. Machree.  Why did she
>       do it?  And how do you know?

>           AMOS
>       She used the steam iron to kill him because
>       she loved him, and he paid attention only
>       to the younger girls.

>           ANJANETTE
>       But, but I never suspected she felt that
>       way about Benjamin...

>           AMOS
>           (shrugs)
>       That's why I'm the detective and you're
>       the designer.

At that moment in come two lovely models (about 5'9") who
stand in the middle of the room with their arms out, waiting.

>           ANJANETTE
>       Ah, here's the meat.

She goes to the fabric racks and brings out two flings.
She begins to throw them on the girls, and the girls, in
bikinis or slips, take it all in stride.

Amos watches.  In a moment the door opens again and a tall,
burly good-looking man in tight T-shirt and jeans comes in.
He has a hankie knotted around his forehead like a stevedore.
His name is FERGIE.

>           FERGIE
>       Forsooth and touché, there.  Never worry
>       and never fear, your boy rag-picker Fergie's
>       here.

63    ANOTHER SHOT  ON FERGIE  AMOS IN MID-B.G.

as Amos watches him.  Fergie heads for the rag barrel.

>                    ANJANETTE
>                   (nervously)
>       There's nothing for you today, Fergie.

>                     FERGIE
>                (points to full
>                     barrel)
>       An idle remark, my lovely queen,
>       When there are obviously remains to be seen.

Amos winces at the bad poetry, but he watches the scene.
Anjanette tries to head him off, but Fergie has the barrel
up and is starting to pack it off.

>                   ANJANETTE
>       Ah, no!  No, we uh need those rags,
>       Fergie, we uh--

>                     FERGIE
>       I'll sell these rags to pay the rent.
>       Fergie's been here, and he just went.

He leaves before Anjanette can stop him.  He was like a
cyclone--in and out--with bad rhymes.  She tries to regain
her composure, and returns to draping the models.

>                   ANJANETTE
>       We're trying for a more animated
>       silhouette this year...the "living"
>       skirt, a skirt that moves, you see.
>       Feminine, ladylike lines.

But Amos is looking after Fergie.  There are thoughts
running through his head.

>                     AMOS
>       Thanks.  When I buy my next original,
>       I'll remember that.

He hurriedly leaves.

64    INT. GLORY LEE WORKROOMS  MED. SHOT ON AMOS

as he comes out of the design room.  Keekee Lee is standing
and talking to Les.  Amos comes up to them in F.G.

>                     AMOS
>       This, uh, Fergie, the man who takes
>       the rags away.  Where does he take
>       them?

65    2-SHOT  AMOS & KEEKEE LEE

                        KEEKEE
            Down to the service alley and
            into a truck; and then they're
            taken to a warehouse downtown.
            Why?

                        AMOS
            Just an idea...Les, come on.

He starts away hurriedly, without even saying goodbye and
Les, tipping his hat, follows. CAMERA HOLDS on them going
down the aisle between sewing machines and to the exit.

                        DISSOLVE TO:

66    INT. ALLEY  ESTABLISHING  DAY

a big battered truck backed up to the loading platform.
Fergie is starting to dump the rags into the truck.  Amos
and Les come out through the doors.

                        AMOS
            Hold it, Fergie.

                        FERGIE
            Good morrow, my man.
            Watch me empty my can.

                        AMOS
            Don't dump it, Fergie, I want to
            talk to you.

Fergie continues starting to dump, as though he wants
the rags in the truck.

                        FERGIE
            Time does not wait,
            And I gotta haul freight.

Amos tries to stop him, Fergie swings, Amos decks him.

                        AMOS
            Are they in the truck, Fergie, or did
            you remove them already?

                        FERGIE
            I've concluded thou art a scurvy lout,
            and I don't know what you're talkin' about.

Amos motions Les to hold his gun on Fergie, and then
Amos searches Fergie, frisking him thoroughly.

67    CLOSE SHOT    AMOS & FERGIE, LES IN B.G.

as Amos pulls a folded sheaf of papers from Fergie's pocket.
He opens them and CAMERA SHOWS us that they are dress designs.

> AMOS
> That's what I figured.  The copies
> of the dress designs were dropped
> in with the scrap rags, and you
> carried them out unnoticed.

> FERGIE
> I meet
> De-feat.

> AMOS
> Then where do you take them, Fergie.

> FERGIE
> I am regal in my silence.

Amos hauls him to his feet.

> AMOS
> Let's get him downtown, Les.  He'll
> talk.

They walk TOWARD CAMERA.

> FERGIE
> You can make me walk,
> But I'll never talk.

SHARP CUT TO:

68    INT. AMOS' OFFICE    ESTABLISHING   EVENING

CLOSEUP on Mrs. Machree in a chair facing Amos.    CAMERA PULLS BACK.

> MRS. MACHREE
> I'll never talk, copper.  I'm no
> stoolie!  I'm innocent, this is
> a lousy frame!

> AMOS
> (to Tim)
> Did you stop off at her house?

Tim holds up the ruined dress KeeKee Lee had given Mrs.
Machree in Scene 28.

> TIM
> Here it is.

(CONTINUED)

68    CONTINUED:

                              AMOS
                    And the steam iron?

Tim holds that up as well.

                              AMOS
                         (continues)
                    Okay.  Trot them both over to McCloud.
                    The dress for a thorough stain analysis,
                    and the steam iron for prints.
                         (beat)
                    You got Mrs. Machree's prints?

                              MRS. MACHREE
                         (holds up inky fingers)
                    He sure as...he sure did, copper!  You'll
                    hear from my mouthpiece about this!

                              AMOS
                         (grinning)
                    Okay, Tim.  Take off.

Tim leaves.  Amos turns to Mrs. Machree.

                              MRS. MACHREE
                    I'll have your badge for this, flatfoot!

                              AMOS
                         (suavely, gentle)
                    Mrs. Machree, how would you like to
                    help me solve a murder?

Her expression changes.  She's a little old lady once more,
involved in a mystery.

                              MRS. MACHREE
                    Ben Glory's killer?

                              AMOS
                    Right on the nose.  My arresting you
                    was a cover-up.  I had to find a
                    sharp and blunt instrument with starch
                    on it, that was used as the murder
                    weapon, and I remembered KeeKee Lee
                    yelling at you about a stained garment.
                    It all fitted.  But I had to get the
                    steam iron out without alarming the
                    real killer.

                              MRS. MACHREE
                    And you think you'll get prints off it?

                                             (CONTINUED)

68    CONTINUED: - 2

                        AMOS
         Most likely the only latents we'll
         get will be yours...but I want the
         killer to sweat. We're getting
         close, and I think someone knows it.

                        MRS. MACHREE
         Well, what do you want me to do, Chief?

                        AMOS
         Just go to a movie, or go home and don't
         answer the phone. Let them think we've
         booked you.

                        MRS. MACHREE
         I can go to my daughter-in-law's for
         dinner. What's she having tonight...
         ah, I think this is a fried liver night,
         but in the name of justice, I'll make
         the sacrifice.

                        AMOS
         You're a Princess, Mrs. Machree.

She rises to leave, winks at him flirtatiously.

                        MRS. MACHREE
         You've got a little pazzaz yourself,
         Burke.

She leaves as PHONE rings. Amos, smiling, picks it up.

                        AMOS
         Captain Burke. Hello, Mrs. Glory.
                   (beat)
         Yes, yes...all right, thanks.

He hangs up as Les comes in. Les looks exhausted.

                        LES
         You'll never get that idiot Fergie
         to talk. He just keeps making
         rotten rhymes...when are we going
         to get a few normal ones, Amos?

                        AMOS
         When murder goes out of fashion.
                   (beat)
         Don't worry about it, I think we've
         got another way to track this thing
         down.

69    ANOTHER SHOT ON AMOS

                         AMOS  (CONT.)
               Carlene Glory just called.  She
               remembered something her husband
               said during that phone conversation
               before he went to the Ellison
               Building.

                         LES
               Which was?

                         AMOS
               A name.  Malvin Kimboyd, Jr.  That's
               M-A-L-V-I-N, K-I-M-B-O-Y-D.  Jr. is
               J...

                         LES
                         (cuts in)
               I know, I know.

                         AMOS
               So run it through Motor Vehicle, and
               get me an address.

Les gets up wearily, walks to door.

                         LES
               You're going to be responsible for
               my fallen arches and flat feet.

                         AMOS
               Don't fret.  A few more days, they
               get webbed and drop off.

Les goes.  CAMERA HOLDS on Amos, smiling.

                                        DISSOLVE TO:

70    EXT. DEPARTMENT STORE  STREET  NIGHT  ESTABLISHING

as Rolls pulls up in front of big picture window.  Amos
gets out of car and walks up to window.  In the window
is a slim, youngish man putting clothes on naked dress
models.  Amos stares at him a long moment, then taps on
the window.  The man turns around.  Amos yells.

                         AMOS
               Are you Malvin Kimboyd, Jr.?

Tilted head, quizzical expression, no response.

                                        (CONTINUED)

70    CONTINUED:

                         AMOS
                        (louder)
               Are you Malvin Kimboyd, Jr.?

Nodding of head.  Still quizzical.  Amos shows badge.

                         AMOS
                   (loud and slowly)
              I...am...from...police...I ...want...to...
              talk...to...you...

Kimboyd motions toward front door, and disappears through
drapes at the back of window.  Amos looks toward door,
then walks to it.  CAMERA LONG SHOT down street as Amos
stands before door.  Door opens.  Amos enters.  CAMERA
HOLDS A BEAT then PANS BACK to store window.  In a second
Kimboyd returns, and Amos is with him.  They talk in
exaggerated pantomime for a few seconds as CAMERA MOVES IN.

71    INT. STORE WINDOW  NIGHT

We are now INSIDE THE WINDOW with Amos and Kimboyd.

                         AMOS
             ...so your landlady said you worked
             here...

                        MALVIN
             But that doesn't explain why you're
             looking for me.

NOTE: Malvin Kimboyd, Jr. is a whack.  Flat out, that's
        the truth of it.  His voice rises as he talks so
that by the end of the speech he is literally trembling
with vibrato.  There is even something a little effeminate
about him, but not much.  And he makes random noises like
whistles and hums and chirrups, as though he's getting
messages from...out there somewhere.

                         AMOS
             I want a name, Mr. Kimboyd.  The name
             of the party you've been passing the
             Glory Lee designs to.

                        MALVIN
                   (weirdly)
            Whoooo...I started out as a thimble,
            but now I'm an egg.

He crouches down, hands wrapped around knees.  Amos stares
unbelievingly.  Then he bends down to talk to Kimboyd.

                           (CONTINUED)

71   CONTINUED:

                    AMOS
                  (gently)
          Well, turn your electric blankie up
          to 9 and just try to forget the
          whole nasty business.

                    MALVIN
                  (whispering)
          But I'm a balance egg...very high in
          poly-unsaturates, very low in cholesterols.

                    AMOS
                  (to himself)
          I've heard of men cracking under
          interrogation, but this is ridiculous.

Kimboyd leaps up, puts hands on hips.

                    MALVIN
          I'm a little teapot, short and stout
                  (looks at one arm)
          here is my handle
                  (looks at other)
          here is my...well whaddaya know, I'm
          a sugar bowl.

                    AMOS
                  (at rope's end)
          Okay, Kimboyd, knock it off!

Kimboyd, like a setter, listens.

                    MALVIN
                  (sounds like a
                    theremin)
          Whooo...whooo...blue is the secret,
          just blue...blue as blue can be...

                    AMOS
                  (furious)
          Your eye'll be <u>black</u> and blue, Kimboyd,
          if you don't come back to earth.

                    MALVIN
          I am a great man, I see in greens and
          wets and hard yellow noises, bang!
          There it goes, flying overhead.

                    AMOS
          What's your contacts name, Kimboyd!
          Come on, Fergie told us you were his
          cohort in this thing.  Now who put
          the designs in the rag barrel?

                                        (CONTINUED)

71    CONTINUED: - 2

Kimboyd begins furiously dressing the dummies, humming and
singing and carrying on in general like some kinda nut.

                    MALVIN
          Oh, lysurgic acid, wherefore art thou,
          LSD, baby chickie sweetie honey doll...

Amos realizes.

                    AMOS
          How long have you been on LSD, Kimboyd?

                    MALVIN
          Whooooooooeeeeee...!

Kimboyd bounds about the dummies, dressing them, decorating
the window.  Amos ducks and weaves and bobs to stay out of
his way.

72    REVERSE ANGLE    THRU PLATE GLASS WINDOW

at the incredulous crowd that is gathering, staring.

73    SAME AS 72

as Amos tries to stay out of Kimboyd's way.

                    MALVIN
          The name you seek, oh purple and pink,
          is Mortimer Gunkman...ah, the name
          falls from the lips like quicksilver...
          wheeeeeee...

                    AMOS
          Mortimer Gunkman?  Who is he, Kimboyd?

                    MALVIN
          Lovelytogs, Lovelytogs, Lovelytogs...

He keeps shrieking the name as he begins donning clothes
himself...a purse, a hat, a dress, whatever...  Amos
suddenly realizes he is being watched, and looks over
his shoulder at

74    INTERCUT  SAME AS 73

the crowd who stare wide-eyed.  Amos does a take, and
begins to edge out of the window as we hear Kimboyd's
lunatic laugh and the word "Lovelytogs" over and over
until we
                              FLOPOVER: TO:

75   CLOSEUP   DOORWAY   NEXT DAY

a **very** **modern!** glass showroom doorway, with the one word
LOVELYTOGS in extremely readable print.  CAMERA PULLS BACK
to show us we are in a hallway of a modern building such
as the California Apparel Mart (110 E. 9th, L.A.), with
many different doorways, all sporting the names of various
firms, and clothing racks being wheeled down the hall, and
models walking back and forth as Amos and Les walk up to
the door.  They look around at the posh building.

>                    LES
>        You say a "knock-off" house is sort
>        of a second-class schlock operation?

>                    AMOS
>        That's what it means in the industry.

>                    LES
>        I wouldn't mind living here myself.

>                    AMOS
>        You can't afford it on your salary.
>        Besides, what would they say if you
>        moved out of the Old Cop's Home?

Les is about to answer when they suddenly hear the SOUND of
GLASS CRASHING and BODIES FALLING and RIOT IMPENDING.

>                    KEEKEE'S VOICE O.S.
>        You aren't going to kill me like you
>        killed Benjamin Glory!

Another crash, louder.

>                    KEEKEE'S VOICE O.S.
>        This half of Glory Lee is harder to kill,
>        Gunkman!

And as Amos and Les stand there, a shadow approaches on the
inside of the glass door, and as they leap back, a body
comes whirling whipping spinning crashing through the
plate-glass door, amid a shower of splinters.  The man
falls flat-out, rolls over and stares up at them.

>                    AMOS
>                 (looking down)
>        Uh, Mortimer Gunkman?

>                    MORTIMER
>                 (smiles incongruously)
>        Why, how kind of you to stop by and say
>        hello.
>                 (beat)
>        Hello.

He faints.  HOLD ON Amos & Les staring as we      FADE OUT.

ACT IV


FADE IN:

76    INT. LOVELYTOGS SHOWROOM   ESTABLISHING   DAY

Gunkman is laid out on a plush sofa.  The showroom is
decorated in modern; deep rugs, mirrors, clothing racks
built into the walls, a few dummies with clothes on them,
and in the middle of the room, a dummy lying on the floor
barely wearing a ripped dress, and the head stomped in.
KeeKee Lee stands, arms akimbo, waiting for another lick
at Gunkman.  Amos and Les stand between them.  Gunkman is
a little, balding fellow, wearing a checkered vest and a
large sticking-plaster across his forehead.

                    KEEKEE
                   (boiling)
          Lemme at him!  I'll pulverize him!

                    MORTIMER AMOS
          Keep away from him, Miss Lee.

                    MORTIMER
                   (repeats)
          Keep away from him, Miss Lee.

                    KEEKEE
          This morning, one of our fabric salesmen,
          Joe Goray, came in to tell me Gunkman
          had copied our cocktail sheath.  I didn't
          know who the thief was yesterday, but
          today I know, and I'm not going to let
          this little rodent get away with it!

                    AMOS
          I found out it was Gunkman last night,
          from a window dresser named Kimboyd.

                    MORTIMER
                   (repeats)
          A window dresser.  Named Kimboyd!

                    AMOS
          I'm paid to handle this kind of thing,
          Miss Lee.  If you have a complaint
          against Gunkman, swear out a warrent.

                              (CONTINUED)

76    CONTINUED:

> MORTIMER
> (repeats)
> Swear out a warrant!  Swear it out!

> KEEKEE
> (lunging)
> Listen to the little fink!  He even copies
> what everybody says.  Hasn't got an original
> thought in his soft head!

Les catches her.  She tries to kick out at Gunkman, who
winces and huddles up in a little ball on the sofa.

> MORTIMER
> (repeats, surly)
> An original thought, hmmph!

> AMOS
> You accused him of killing Ben Glory.

> KEEKEE
> He must have!  I knew Ben was determined
> to ruin whoever stole those designs.  So
> he found out it was Gunkman, and Gunkman
> killed him to save his neck.

> MORTIMER
> Gunkman killed him?  To save his neck?

77    ANOTHER SHOT  PAST KEEKEE TO AMOS & MORTIMER

Amos leans over him.

> AMOS
> It looks bad, Gunkman.

> MORTIMER
> Looks bad.

> AMOS
> You'd better talk.

> MORTIMER
> Talk.  Better.

> AMOS
> Who was your contact at the Glory Lee
> factory?  As if I didn't know.

> MORTIMER
> You know.

(CONTINUED)

77    CONTINUED:

                    AMOS
        It was Anjanette Delacroix, wasn't it,
        Gunkman?

                    MORTIMER
        Anjanette Delacroix.

                    KEEKEE
        Anjanette?  But she's been with Glory
        Lee almost as long as we've been in
        business.  She makes a fantastic salary.
        There's no sense to it.  Why?

                    AMOS
        Well, Gunkman?  Why?

                    MORTIMER
        Why...uh...er...

                    KEEKEE
                (rudely)
        If it means he has to come up with an
        original thought, we'll be here till
        we're covered with dust.

                    AMOS
        She needed money, right Gunkman?
                (beat)
        Or it was reveng...how about that?
                (beat)
        You were having an affair with her...
        you blackmailed her, somehow.

                    MORTIMER
        Yes.

                    AMOS
        Yes what?  Which one?

                    MORTIMER
        One.

                    AMOS
        One.  The first reason?  She needed
        money?

Gunkman nods.  Amos has slipped into a mad scene with
him, trying to pry information loose.  It has become a
charade.

                    AMOS
        She needed money, right?  For what?

78    ANOTHER SHOT   GUNKMAN & AMOS, KEEKEE & LES IN B.G.

Gunkman begins pantomiming the dealing of cards.

> AMOS
> (guessing)
> Uh...washing dishes...no...peeling a
> banana...

Gunkman shuffles, cuts, deals cards around him.

> AMOS
> (continues)
> Uh...cards...playing cards...she was
> gambling...she needed the money to
> cover gambling debts!

Gunkman touches his nose, meaning "on the nose, you've
got it." (NOTE: all the stylistic tricks of the TV charade
games should be used, magnified and parodied here.)

> AMOS
> (continues)
> Gambling with who?  She was in debt
> gambling to who, Gunkman?

Gunkman has risen off the sofa by now, and the other three
are seated as he plays the game. He now begins opening an
invisible box, and eating something.

> KEEKEE
> Can...uh, container...no, box...BOX!

Gunkman smiles, points to her, she got it.

> LES
> XBX She was gambling with a box?

Amos and KeeKee and Gunkman stare at Les sourly.

> LES
> (apologetic)
> Sorry...

> AMOS
> (trying again)
> Box...big box...little box...it's
> bigger than a bread box...it's self-
> employed...it's a dealer in services
> ...it's John Cameron Swayze...no...

Gunkman keeps eating, licking his lips, selecting one after
another of whatever it is, from the box he holds.

                              (CONTINUED)

78    CONTINUED:

> AMOS
> (continues)
> You're eating something...pickles,
> dill pickles, sweet pickles, cucumber
> pickles, cucumbers...peanuts, pistachio
> nuts, cashews...

> LES
> Gesundheit...

> AMOS
> (madly)
> Avocodos...cumquats...papaya slices...
> candy...chocolate creams...butter—

Gunkman cuts him off.  He signals wildly it is "candy".

> AMOS
> Candy!  It's candy in a box.

> LES
> Candy Box?

> AMOS
> Candy...no, it's Candy Sturtevant!  The
> gambler!  Is that it Gunkman?  Candy
> Sturtevant, she was in hock to him?

Gunkman nods.

> MORTIMER
> Candy Sturtevant.
> (holds hand up to
> neck indicating
> height)
> In hock.

Amos nods.  The conversation is ended.  He knows what he
needs to know.

> AMOS
> I'm sure Miss Lee will have some papers
> delivered to you, Mr. Gunkman, by way
> of the City Attorney's Office.  I'd
> advise you not to leave town...we might
> decide you had something to do with the
> murder of Benjamin Glory.

> MORTIMER
> Don't leave town.

                                    (CONTINUED)

78    CONTINUED: - 2

Amos takes KeeKee Lee's arm, and the three of them start to
leave through the shattered plate-glass door.  Amos pauses.

                    AMOS
          You can say that again.

                    MORTIMER
          Don't leave town.

Amos and Les give Gunkman an exhausted look.  They open the
door.  KeeKee pauses and turns back to Gunkman.

                    KEEKEE
          Copycat!

                    MORTIMER
                    (grins)
          Yeah, how about that!

Amos slams door.  CAMERA HOLDS on Gunkman, jaunty, jolly.

                              DISSOLVE TO:

79    EXT. STREET   ROLLING SHOT (STOCK)   DAY

      as Rolls passes through.

80    INT. ROLLS   (PROCESS)   DAY

      Amos and Tim in back seat, Les & Henry in front.

                    AMOS
          All right, now what's so urgent
          that we had to pick you up?

                    TIM
          Something Anjanette Delacroix said to
          me didn't ring true.  The first time
          I spoke to her, she told me she was
          from Switzerland.

                    LES
          She is.

                    TIM
          Maybe, just maybe.  She said she was
          from St. Gallen, near Lake Zurich,
          but her accent was French.

                    AMOS
          So what, there are thousands of
          French-speaking Swiss.  France
          borders Switzerland on the west.

                              (CONTINUED)

80    CONTINUED:

                         TIM
          Right, there are French-speaking
          people in Switzerland.  But of
          the five million, four hundred
          and twenty-nine thousand and sixty-
          one people in Switzerland, 69.3%
          spoke German, only 18.9% spoke
          French and the rest other languages.

                         AMOS
                       (dryly)
          Fascinating.

                         TIM
          Captain, French is only spoken in
          5 of the "cantons" or states, of
          Switzerland, and St. Gallen isn't
          one of them.  It's one of the few
          cantons, in fact, where German is
          spoken as the only language.

                         LES
          It's possible, though.

                         TIM
          Sure, anything's possible, but it
          didn't sing right for me, so I
          checked out her naturalization
          papers.
                       (beat)
          She's French, Captain.  All the
          way.  From Paris.

                         AMOS
          Why would she lie about it, hmmm.

                         LES
          Hiding something.

                         AMOS
                       (flatly)
          Interpol needs a cunning mind like
          yours.
                       (beat)
          This is all too pat.  Everything points
          at Anjanette Delacroix.  The selling of
          designs, the lying about her nationality,
          her daughter about to be kept by Glory.
          Too pat.

                                   (CONTINUED)

80    CONTINUED: - 2

                         TIM
          What do you mean "too pat", Captain.
          It looks like she's the killer.

                         AMOS
          Yes, that's the trouble.  There's no
          real motive for a killing.

                         LES
          But if Glory was on to her thefts...

                         AMOS
          No, not nearly enough.  Here was a man
          who put her to work when she first
          came to this country, she thought he
          was a saint...she wouldn't kill him.
                         (beat)
          There's something missing.

                         TIM
          But if all the clues point to her, sir...

                         AMOS
          Yeah, that's it.  Every time we hit one
          of these twisty cases, and all the clues
          point to only one suspect, it always
          turns out it was the one you suspected
          least.

     Tim and Les nod at this.  How true.  31 weeks of true.

                         AMOS
                         (continues)
          Well, this time we're going to find out
          who that least-suspected party really
          is!  This time we're not going to be
          fooled by the obvious solution!
                         (beat)
          Tim, we'll drop you off at the office.
          I want you to call a friend of mine.

                         TIM
                         (takes out pad)
          Who's that, sir?

                         AMOS
          Inspector Javert (pronounced: Jah-vair)
          of the French Sureté (suhr-et-ay).

                         LES
          And what wm will we be doing?

                                        (CONTINUED)

80    CONTINUED: - 3

                         AMOS
          Locating Candy Sturtevant.

                         LES
                       (incredulous)
          Candy Sturtevant?  Don't put me on,
          Amos.  No one can find him.  No one's
          even met him.  He's the gambling king
          of this city and he's never been
          pinched, we don't even have a description
          of him.

                         AMOS
          But you and I will find him.  And we'll
          get into whatever game he has going
          tonight.  I need to know what Anjanette
          Delacroix wanted money for.

                         LES
          And precisely how do you propose to do
          that?  Just walk up to somebody on the
          street and say I want to find Candy
          Sturtevant?

                                        SHARP FLOPOVER TO:

81    EXT. STREET/NEWSSTAND   DAY    ESTABLISHING

      the newsstand is a block long, one of those outdoor jobs
       with the racks on the empty wall of a building.  The
      Rolls is parked at the curb as Amos approaches THIRTY,
      THE NEWSIE.  Les walks with Amos.  Thirty is a very
      studious-looking type, with horn-rimmed glasses, a thatch
      of hair, and a semi-scurrying look, like a smart rodent.
      CAMERA ZOOMS IN as Amos comes face-to-face with Thirty.

                         AMOS
          I want to find Candy Sturtevant, Thirty.

                         THIRTY
          Oh, sure, Captain Burke.  For a fellow
          lover of pre-Colombian art, nothing is
          impossible.  Just let me check.

      He lays down his papers, rolls up his pant leg and from his
      garter takes a small black book.  He leafs through it.

                         THIRTY
          The game tonight will be...

      As he speaks, CAMERA MOVES IN on Les' incredulous face and
      Amos smug expression as we suddenly
                                        SHARP CUT TO:

82    EXT. STREET ESTABLISHING    NIGHT

an EXTREMELY HIGH SHOT down on a deserted street and an alley.
CAMERA COMES DOWN to alley mouth, where it picks up CLOSEUP
of Amos and Les, skulking in the mouth of the alley, waiting.
They are dressed like a pair of bums.  Droopy squash hats,
old suits, thoroughly scuddy-looking.

                    AMOS
          You made sure there's no xxx identification
          on you, no papers, no bdage?

                    LES
          I'm clean, Amos, but I still think this
          is a false hope.  Sturtevant is the mystery
          man of the underworld.  The D.A.'s office
          has been trying to raid one of his games
          for months, and they can't even find him.

At that moment, the SOUND of a huge truck.

83    ANGLE DOWN STREET    NIGHT

as a gigantic aluminum-bodied moving van cruises slowly
into the street, its headlights shining.  As it passes,
slowly, Amos and Les run out of the alley, jump on the
rear deck platform, and grab onto the handles.

84    CLOSEUP  REAR OF MOVING VAN (PROCESS)  NIGHT

as the streets move past slowly, CAMERA HOLDS on Amos and
Les up against rear of van.  Amos knocks three-one-two on
the steel window.  It opens.  A dark face inside looks out.

                    AMOS
                  (reciting)
          "Mary had a little lamb,
          "And the doctor fainted."

The window closes, and after a moment, the door opens.  Amos
and Les slip inside.

85    INT. MOVING VAN  ESTABLISHING

If we didn't know we were inside a moving van coursing thru
the streets, we'd think it was a New Orleans gambling house.
A dice table, roulette wheel, poker table, blackjack counter.
A bar.  The works.  Very plush, velvet drapes, deep rugs, no
windows, soft music, pretty girls in short skirts moving thru
with trays of drinks.  A very high-class brand of clientele.
A gambling joint on wheels.  Amos and Les are very much out
of place.  They stare unbelievingly.  It's amazing!

                                        (CONTINUED)

74

85   CONTINUED:

A tall, slim, extremely beautiful girl wearing tight gold
lamé capris comes toward them.  She wears a mask covering
her eyes--the traditional domino--and she is quite a pack
of action with her high-coiffed platinum hair.  She reaches
them and surveys them.  The girl is CANDY STURTEVANT.

                    CANDY
          Eccch!  You two are filthy!  How
          did you find out about the game?

                    AMOS
          A friend in low places.

                    CANDY
          We don't deal in places that low.

                    AMOS
          We're not here to gamble, in any case.
          We'd like some information.

                    CANDY
          I truly dislike upsetting your conception
          of the ethical structure of the universe,
          friend, but this is not the Christian
          Science Reading Room.

                    AMOS
          Do you know Anjanette Delacroix?

                    CANDY
               (suspicious)
          Precisely who are you?

                    LES
          Perhaps we'd better talk to the boss.
          Is Mr. Sturtevant here?

                    CANDY
          There is no Mr. Sturtevant.

                    LES
          Candy Sturtevant?  There isn't any
          Candy Sturtevant?

                    CANDY
          I didn't say that.

                    LES
          But you said there was no...

                              (CONTINUED)

85    CONTINUED: - 2

                    AMOS
         No wonder they couldn't find you.
         They were looking for a man.

                    CANDY
         I'm a woman.

                    AMOS
         I'll go along with that.

                    LES
         What a picture to hang in the Post Office!

                    CANDY
         You have three seconds to tell me what
         you want, and who you are, before I have
         two very ugly gentlemen named Angie and
         Claude play reupholster your faces.

                    AMOS
                 (logically)
         We're from the Better Business Bureau.

                    CANDY
         You look like stewbums, but I think you're
         trouble.

                    AMOS
         Not unless you make us be trouble.

                    CANDY
         You're related to Teddy Roosevelt.
         (pronounced: Roe-zeh-velt, not Roo...)

                    LES
         What?

                    CANDY
         You walk softly, smell bad, and carry a
         big stick.

                    AMOS
         One question, and we vanish into the
         night like the Arabs, tent and all.

                    CANDY
                 (holding nose)
         Smell and all will be sufficient.

                    LES
         I knew we were too authentic.
                                    (CONTINUED)

85    CONTINUED: - 3

> AMOS
> Anjanette Delacroix.  She was in
> debt to you.  Quite a pile.  Why?

> CANDY
> Because she's a lousy blackjack
> player, and a worse roulette player,
> and at the dice table she's a natural
> disaster area.

> AMOS
> No...why did she gamble?

> CANDY
> Give me a hundred and eighteen good
> reasons why I should stand here jawing
> with you when Angie and Claude are
> fairly frothing to work?

> AMOS
> Do you want the list alphapetical or
> chronological?

> CANDY
> That tears it!
> (yells over
> shoulder)
> Angie!  Claude!  Playtime!

Two huge ape-like hulks in tuxedos emerge from the throng,
bulging, and advance on Amos and Les.  They come in at
right angles and Amos takes his out with a feint left, a
right to the gut and a judo chop to the Adam's Apple.  Les
stands his ground as the other orangutan comes at him,
almost like a matador passing a bull, and as the hulk throws
a left, Les moves his head slightly.  The fist passes Les'
head and thunks into the metal wall of the moving van.  The
ape clutches his hand, sucks his knuckles and begins to
cry.  Candy comes over, slaps him.

> CANDY
> G'wan, you big crybaby, get outta here!
> (to crowd)
> All right, troops, just mind the boards;
> nothing's happening.

The crowd goes back to the action.

> AMOS
> (to Les)
> That was very nice, that duck and bob.

(CONTINUED)

85    CONTINUED: - 4

> LES
> Really?  Why, thanks, Amos.  It's
> a modification of ki-ya (pronounced:
> kye-yah) by way of an old karate
> defense.  But you were nice, too.
> I really liked that judo cut...haven't
> seen it used in years.

> AMOS
> (chattily)
> Yes, it is nice, isn't it.  Too bad
> more officers don't use it.

> LES
> We'll have to work out at the gym,
> exchange a few pet holds...

Candy has been standing behind them, listening to all this.
Now she shoves them apart.

> CANDY
> All right, you two; you sound like a
> pair of Pasadena housewives exchanging
> recipes.  Who the devil are you?
> (beat)
> And can you use a job?

> AMOS
> We're from the police.

> CANDY
> (shrilly)
> Queep!

> AMOS
> Don't worry about it.  We aren't here
> to bust you.  That's another department's
> job.

> LES
> (pleasantly)
> Perhaps some other time.

> AMOS
> All we want now is something on Anjanette
> Delacroix.

> CANDY
> She ran up some pretty stiff losses
> trying to get money for her daughter.
> We talked one night, she seemed the
> wrong sort to be spreading herself
> so thin, and I got most of it out of
> (MORE)

(CONTINUED)

85     CONTINUED: - 5

CANDY (CONT'D.)
her.  A real self-indulgent kid, her
daughter.  Wanted everything too rich
for her blood.  The mother didn't want
to give, the daughter started getting
pretty wild and hanging around men the
mother said were losers.

AMOS
Glory.

CANDY
Yeah, she mentioned the name.  Worked
for him.  Well, she started paying back
what she owed me, and another couple
grand, she'll be square.

LES
She hasn't paid it all back yet?

Candy shakes her head no.  Amos and Les look at each other.

AMOS
No one kills the goose before all the
golden eggs have been extracted.
(beat)
She didn't do it.  No sense to it.

CANDY
You're, uh, from the police, huh?
(they nod)
Well, it was mysterious while it
lasted.  I suppose I'll be put out of
business now.

LES
What the Good Captain was trying to
tell you, Miss Sturtevant, is that by
some obscure code of ethics, he has
not come here to mobilize the jernt.
And if I were you, I wouldn't worry.
It seems to me the D.A.'s office has
been singularly ineffectual in raiding
your operation.

At which point there is the SOUND of squealing brakes, the
van slams to a halt, tables fall over, the back door bursts
open and the gambling casino is loaded with plainclothes
and uniformed police.  Rifles and riot guns at the ready,
they move in noisily.  The LEAD COP speaks.

LEAD COP
All right, you big spenders!  Put 'em
where we can see 'em!

86   3⚊SHOT   AMOS, CANDY & LES

The men are surprised, confused; Candy is furious. She rips off her mask, flings it down.

>                    CANDY
>           Never trust a cop! You...you...crooks!

>                     LES
>           We're innocent! We didn't know a thing
>           about it!

The police start hustling the patrons from the van, into a waiting black mariah seen THRU BACK DOOR. Two cops come up to Amos and Les and Candy.

>                  LEAD COP
>           All right, you two, wet brains, let's
>           go.

>                     LES
>           Hey, wait a minute, we're not...

>                    AMOS
>                  (smugly)
>           No, no, officer, you see, I'm...

>                   CANDY
>                 (interrupts)
>           He's Candy Sturtevant, the mysterious
>           gambling czar! In disguise! Nab him!

The two cops throw down on Amos, while he fumfuhs and tries to find words.

>                   AMOS
>           But I'm Captain Amos Burke. The Captain
>           from Homicide...

>                     LES
>           The one with the Rolls-Royce!

>                  LEAD COP
>           Sure, and I'm Little Orphan Annie.
>           Only I left my blank eyeballs in my
>           other suit. Move out!

The two derelicts move out at gunpoint as Candy Sturtevant laughs behind them. CAMERA HOLDS on her as she laughs, till something makes her stop laughing, and as CAMERA PULLS BACK we see another cop slapping cuffs on her.

>                              SHARP CUT TO:

87    INT. AMOSIXS HOMICIDE OFFICE   ESTABLISHING   NIGHT

CLOSEUP on Tim and lovely SGT. AMES sipping a malted together.
One malted, two straws.

                    SGT. AMES
          A girl would be a fool to turn down
          a madcap spendthrift like you.

                    TIM
          I have blue eyes.

                    SGT. AMES
          So has a koala bear.

                    TIM
          I'm a good dancer.

                    SGT. AMES
          You're every girl's dream of romance.

                    TIM
          You've been spoiled rotten by Captain
          Burke's debonair, worldly manner.

A misty look comes into Sgt. Ames' eyes.

                    SGT. AMES
          Well, you have to admit: there is a
          man who does everything right.  Never
          a foul-up, never a misstep, never a
          wrong number...

PHONE RINGS.  Sgt. Ames picks it up.

                    SGT. AMES
          Homicide, Sgt. Ames speaking.
                    (beat)
          Why, hello there, Captain.  I was just
          taking your name in vain.
                    (she listens)
          They allowed you one call?  Who allowed
          you one call?
                    (beat)
          You're what?  You're where?  Y-y-essir,
          yessir, yes, right away, sir...

She hangs up, looks at Tim with a lost expression.

                    SGT. AMES
                    (continues)
          Chicken Little, the sky is falling...

Tim looks at her bewildered expression; her distant voice.

                              (CONTINUED)

87    CONTINUED:

                         TIM
            What's the matter?

                         SGT. AMES
                       (vacantly)
            Don't get lost, good-looking, you
            may turn out to be a winner yet.

                              SHARP CUT TO:

88    INT. DRUNK TANK  ESTABLISHING  NIGHT

      thru the bars at the mass of jammed-together people, with
      Amos and Les and front, as the door swings open and a turnkey
      lets them out.  Tim is laughing.

                         AMOS
                       (furious)
            One more giggle, friend Tilson, and
            you'll be examining sand fleas in
            your uniform out past Pismo Beach.

      Les snorts ruefully, and follows Amos as they stalk away.
      CAMERA HOLDS on Tim, snickering, trying to hold it back,
      as he follows.

                              SHARP CUT TO:

89    INT. AMOS' OFFICE  ESTABLISHING    NIGHT

      as the three men come through the door.  Amos goes to his
      desk.  Les slams the door, Tim smiles boyishly.

                         AMOS
            So they were assigned out of the
            District Attorney's office and
            they didn't know us.  So what?
            What have you got on the Glory
            Lee problem?

                         TIM
            You were right, sir.  Inspector
            Javert of the French Sureté checked
            the records.  Just as you'd suggested;
            the dates matched almost to the month.
                       (beat)
            And the stains on the dress, they were
            blood.  Type O-Negative, same as Benjamin
            Glory's.  He was killed with that steam
            iron.  No other prints, just Mrs. Machree's.

                              (CONTINUED)

89   CONTINUED:

                        AMOS
             Well, that cinches it.

                        LES
             Cinches what?

                        AMOS
             I'm glad we waited, that we didn't bite
             on the obvious clues pointing all to
             the same person; that we ferreted out
             hidden facts that showed us who the
             real killer is, the one we least-suspected!

                        LES & TIM
                        (together)
             Who?

                                        SHARP CUT TO:

90   INT. SABLE'S APARTMENT  ESTABLISHING  NIGHT

     CLOSEUP 2-SHOT on Amos & Anjanette Delacroix.  Sable, Les
     and Tim in background, reflected in the many mirrors.

                        AMOS
             Anjanette Delacroix, I arrest you for
             the murder of Benjamin Glory.

                        ANJANETTE
             You are wrong, you are crazy!

     Amos shows her the Colonel's eagle.

                        AMOS
             This was in Benjamin Glory's pocket.
             An eagle from a United States Army
             Colonel's uniform.  There's just
             such a uniform hanging in the closet
             in that other room...
                        (he gestures)
             ...but both the insignia are there.

                        SABLE
             So what does that mean!  It could have
             come from anywhere.

                        AMOS
             But it didn't.  It was Glory's, and it
             was an older one.  One that he had had
             years before, and had somehow given to
             the person that killed him.

                                        (CONTINUED)

90    CONTINUED:

                          ANJANETTE
            But I did not know him before I
            came to this country from Switzer--

                          AMOS
            You're not from Switzerland. You're
            French. And you knew Benjamin Glory
            when he was a Colonel in the occupation
            forces.
                      (beat)
            We know you killed him. A random print
            on the steam iron you used.

                          SABLE
                      (gasps)
            Oh! Mother!

Anjanette's face crumbles. She has come too far...she sinks down.

                          ANJANETTE
                      (softly)
            I'm so tired...so very tired...
                      (beat)
            I was so young, I never knew love, from
            the first moment I was able to understand
            love, the Bosch, the filthy Nazis were
            there...and then came the Americans, and
            Benjamin.
                      (sadly)
            He told me he loved me...I-I was not that
            kind of girl, I was a good girl, but we
            made love, and he gave me his eagle, and
            told me he would come back for me after
            the war.

Sable comes to her mother, touches her.

91    CLOSEUP   ANJANETTE

the weary desolate look of too many years of lies.

                          ANJANETTE
                      (continues)
            But he never came back. And then I found
            I was, I was carrying Sable. I thought
            perhaps, perhaps Benjamin was <u>unable</u> to
            get back to me. I worked as a designer,
            made a little money, when Sable was just
            a child, I came with her, here. To be
            near Benjamin.

                                        (CONTINUED)

91  CONTINUED:

                    AMOS
          And you found he had never tried
          to get back, that he was already
          married.

                    ANJANETTE
          He did not even recognize me.  I had
          been a casual flirtation, a--a street
          girl to him.  It had been ten years,
          and I was not even a shadow in his
          mind.

                    AMOS
          So you went to work for him.

                    ANJANETTE
          To be near him.

                    SABLE
          Oh, Mother, I--I never knew...I...

Anjanette holds Sable as the younger woman sinks down
beside her.  She holds her and rubs her hair gently.

                    ANJANETTE
          Shhh.  Shhh, my baby.  It was not too
          bad.  After a while.  I was happy,
          seeing you grow up...

                    SABLE
          XXX      (with horror)
          And then he wanted to...to...this apartment.
          You knew...

                    ANJANETTE
          I had to stop him, somehow.  I gambled
          thinking I could make enough money to
          take us far away, but I only lost, and
          it grew worse.

                    AMOS
          You had to sell the company's secrets
          to get even.

                    ANJANETTE
          And I called him, early in the morning,
          when there was no other way out, and
          told him to come to the office, that I
          knew who was behind the thefts.
                    (MORE)

                              (CONTINUED)

91    CONTINUED: - 2

                          ANJANETTE (CONT'D)
            I told him who I was, who Sable was,
            and I showed him the eagle, so he
            would know I was not lying. I tried
            to show him what a terrible thing he
            would do if he did not leave her alone.
            But he laughed...and hit me.

                          AMOS
            What kind of a monster would laugh.

                          ANJANETTE
                            (bitterly)
            The kind who left a young French girl
            to have her baby in the rubble of a
            dead city. The kind who had covered
            all the years of his sins and rottenness
            by smiles.
                            (beat)
            He accused me of lying, said Sable was
            not his daughter, that I was a woman of
            the streets, and did that sort of
            thing all the time...that...that

She breaks down. Sable comforts her.

                          SABLE
                            (to Amos)
            Stop now! Leave her alone! She isn't
            what you think, she's tired, and she
            only did it out of desperation...

Anjanette's head comes up, her eyes burn fiercely.

                          ANJANETTE
            Yes. Yes! Desperation! He had not
            yet moved into this place...she was
            still safe...I begged him...I had
            worked late, and everyone else was
            gone from the building...

                          AMOS
                            (gently)
            You struck him with the iron...

                          ANJANETTE
            And took the elevator to the fifth
            floor, loaded with dummies, and put
            him in. In the morning I tampered
            with it--yes, they taught us many
            things in the Resistance, even how to
            sabotage machinery--and let it fall.

                                        (CONTINUED)

91   CONTINUED: - 3

> AMOS
>
> Hoping they would think he was
> killed in a faulty elevator crash.

She nods.

> AMOS
> (continues)
> You had no way of knowing he had
> slipped the eagle into his pocket,
> or that the stains on the steam
> iron would cling to the starch residue,
> and come off on Mrs. Machree's work.

She is weeping now, being held by Sable.  Suddenly
Anjanette leaps up, shoves Sable away, streaks for the
penthouse terrace and the balcony...

> ANJANETTE
> (hysterical)
> Finis!  Finis!  Finis!

Tim breaks away and catches her.  She collapses in his
arms, sobbing pitifully, a shattered empty woman.
As Tim helps her toward the door, gently, CAMERA HOLDS
on Sable and Amos.

> AMOS
> (kindly)
> Juries in this country are made up
> of mothers and fathers.  They can
> be made to understand...

She nods, wanly, and turns away.  Les walks off with her,
giving Amos a reassuring nod.  CAMERA HOLDS on Amos as he
turns toward the windows and the night.  As he clicks off
the lights, we see him in shadow, staring out across the
silent terrace.

> DISSOLVE TO:

92   INT. AMOS' HOME  HALLWAY   ESTABLISHING   NIGHT

a MEDIUM LONG SHOT FROM ABOVE as the SOUND of a key in
the lock precedes the opening of the front door, and Amos
comes in, his tie slipped down, his jacket over his
shoulder, the stamp of weariness on his face.  A CLOCK
SOMEWHERE STRIKES TWO A.M.

> DOC'S VOICE O.S.
> Amos...Amos dear, is that you?

93    TRUCKING SHOT  WITH AMOS

as he slings his jacket across the hall table and mulches
into the living room.  CAMERA MOVES AROUND BEHIND HIM as
he enters living room.

> AMOS
> You're kidding!  You've got to be
> kidding...you're still playing?

They are all around the poker table, as before.

> SATCH
> Just finished.  We're now in the
> process of separating the poor
> losers.

> AMOS
> (brightly)
> You mean I now belong to one of you?

They all nod, matter-of-factly.

> AMOS
> (continues)
> Okay, who's the lucky one?

They all turn to stare, as one, at the bar.  CAMERA PANS
TO BAR as we

                                        SHARP CUT TO:

94    MED. CLOSEUP  HENRY AT BAR

in ascot, cigarette in long holder, velvet smoking jacket,
sitting at bar, legs crossed, very dapper, very debonair,
drinking martini.

> HENRY
> (coolly)
> Turn off lights before go to bed,
> Burke.  In morning want oatmeal with
> cinammon, orange juice, coffee and
> two three-minute eggs...or maybe
> three two-minute eggs...have to think
> about it...

> AMOS
> (flabbergasted)
> I'd rather join a monestary!

> HENRY
> Not so much noise, kiddo...want to go
> to sleep.

95  ANOTHER SHOT

as Henry polishes off drink, sets down glass, and sporting
cigarette in holder at rakish angle, perambulates out of
room to LOUD STRAINS of JAPANESE SANDMAN.  CAMERA HOLDS on
Amos Burke, boy servant.

FADE TO BLACK.

FADE OUT.

THE END

Honey Goes Ape!

## Editor's Note: Same Samish, Different Show

While Amos Burke was attempting to rub shoulders with 007 and Napoleon Solo, Four Star Television bought the rights to the *Honey West* book series, issued by Ellison's then-publisher, Pyramid Books. The character, one of the first female private detectives, had debuted in THIS GIRL FOR HIRE, a 1957 novel by husband-and-wife writers Forest and Gloria Fickling—writing as "G.G. Fickling"—and would go on to headline ten more books through 1972.

"They decided to do a female Amos Burke—a hard boiled, pre-*Charlie's Angels* detective—so they hired Annie Francis," recalls Ellison. "I was gonna tell you a great story about Annie Francis," he interjects, "but it turns out it was an Angie Dickinson story." Continuing the *Police Woman* detour, Ellison laughs, "She had a mouth that would make a longshoreman turn white!" before heading back *West*, "Anne Francis was the sweetest woman in the world, just a darling."

ABC introduced West to the television audience in an April 1965 episode of *Burke's Law* before her own eponymous, half-hour series hit the air in September of that year. Ellison—still a Four Star favorite despite his sinking status at ABC (courtesy of Adrian Samish...you really owe it to yourself to pick up a copy of BRAIN MOVIES, Volume 2 for the background on Samish; it's been out for three years, so there's really no excuse)—contributed a teleplay littered with pop culture references ranging from Sonny&Cher to *Lady Chatterley's Lover*. He also took the opportunity to write Francis into a bearskin bikini: "Was the intent of the script to get Anne Francis into a cave woman costume? If someone throws you a delicious papaya, you could wear it as a hat, you could put it on as a hubcap, or you could have Anne Francis dress in it. Never turn down a freebie."

Sadly, the shadow of Samish stretched over the mid-sixties, eclipsing yet another Ellison-scripted opus and Honey never went ape. *Honey West* was cancelled after a single, thirty-episode season, joining *Amos Burke, Secret Agent*—axed mid-season—in the annals of the one-season wonders.

# "HONEY GOES APE!"

FADE IN:

1    MED. LONG SHOT - ON SKY - DAY - HELICOPTER PASSES THRU

CAMERA MOVES IN on chopper as it passes over forest.

2    INT. COPTER - PAST OCCUPANTS TO GROUND BELOW (IN PROCESS)

SAM BOLT is flying the chopper. HONEY WEST beside him.
Behind them three extremely good-looking grey flannel
types: rugged jaws, steely eyes, matinee idols all. They
are the members of the law firm of Contretemps, Bonaventure
& Belial. The copter passes over what is obviously a
large estate. BRUCE BONAVENTURE points.

             BONAVENTURE
    The Ervine Estate. Two hundred acres.

They pass over a huge Chas. Addams-style house at one end
of the estate. CLARK CONTRETEMPS points.

             CONTRETEMPS
    That's the house.

                  (CONTINUED:)

Now they pass over dense forest again, and as they come
low over a clearing, they see a rocky defile, and caves
hewn in the cliffs. There is movement below. BART BELIAL
points and the copter dips down.

             BELIAL
    There's the cave he took her to!

As copter swings lower we see through the lucite ports
a girl crouched over a stone-pit fire. She is wearing an
animal hide. A boy with hair as long as hers comes out
of the cave, and stares up at them. Honey stares down.

             BONAVENTURE
    There they are...that's your assignment.

             HONEY
    Nothing like split-level suburbia, I always
    say.

Copter pulls up as we

la.

2    CONTINUED:

Honey gives him a look.  Of <u>course</u> it's the house, idiot!
They pass over an open plain of short length, and we see
a dozen abandoned oil-pumping rigs.  They are obviously
in disuse, weed-overgrown. Belial points to them.

                    BELIAL
          Used to be a pretty active oilfield,
          but it ran out about ten years ago.
          Dry as a bone now.

*interchange*

Now they pass over dense forest again, and as they come
low over a clearing, they see a rocky defile, and caves
hewn in the cliffs.  There is movement below. BART BELIAL
points again, and the copter dips down.

                    BELIAL
                  (continues)
          There's the cave he took her to!

As copter swings lower, we see through the lucite ports
a girl crouched over a stone-pit fire.  She is wearing an
animal hide.  A boy with hair almost as long as hers
comes out of the cave, and stares up at them.  Honey stares
down.

                    BONAVENTURE
          There they are...that's your assignment.

                    HONEY
          Nothing like split-level suburbia, I always
          say.

Copter pulls up as we

                              HARD CUT TO:

3    CLOSEUP - ON SONNY

the boy with the long hair, also wearing an animal hide. SONNY looks up, sees the copter is buzzing the caves and with a swift movement notches an arrow into a strange wrist-slingshot. CAMERA PAST HIM to the copter near overhead. The girl, CHÉR, rises from the pit-fire, makes a movement to stop him.

                  CHÉR
        Sonny!  Don't!

He looses the arrow.

4    CLOSEUP - THE COPTER

as the arrow sinks into the metal near the lucite ports.

5    INT. COPTER - CLOSE ON SAM

as the metal tip of the arrow comes through the metal skin near his face.  He rears back in anger.

                  SAM
        Anybody see an apple on my head?

                  HONEY
        Set it down in that gulley back there,
        Sam.  We'll trek in.

6    EXT. COPTER - MED. LONG SHOT ON SKY

as copter pulls up and away from caves we PAN LEFT SMOOTHLY and MOVE IN on Sonny & Chér still standing on the ledge. Behind them is a clothesline with animal-skin laundry. Sonny still stares into the sky.  Into CLOSE 2-SHOT.

                  SONNY
        I told 'em to leave us alone or I'd
        make 'em sorry!

                  CHÉR
        If I didn't love you, I'd be upset
        about that nasty streak of yours.
                (beat)
        C'mon, dinner's ready.

She takes a TV dinner off the grating covering the pit-fire, and peels back the tin foil.  They sit and eat as we

                            FLIP-FRAME TO:

7    TRUCKING SHOT – THRU FOREST – CLOSE ON LEGS – DAY

as we see Sam's legs go thru, striking thru tall grass and foliage; then three identical pairs of legs, grey flannel, one after another, differentiated only by the identical black attache cases swinging with legs, one embossed "Bruce Bonaventure", the second "Clark Contretemps", the third "Bart Belial". And after a beat, a <u>very</u> shapely pair of West-style legs, in high heels, having a helluva time in the tall timber. We HEAR their VOICES OVER:

> BELIAL'S VOICE O.S.
> There was some talk about clearing away this forest.

> CONTRETEMPS' VOICE O.S.
> A big office building complex.

> BELIAL'S VOICE O.S.
> Cinema City. But it fell through.

> HONEY'S VOICE O.S.
> (annoyed)
> Probably too much trouble with the dinosaurs...<u>nuts</u>! There goes the <u>other</u> nylon!

> BONAVENTURE'S VOICE O.S.
> It's just a little further.

CAMERA ANGLE RISES and SHOOTS PAST them as Sam brushes aside the last of the foliage and we see across the rocky ground to the ledge and the two kids eating. CAMERA HOLDS TIGHT behind them and MOVES IN with them so we see Sonny and Chér with increasing clarity. They are early twenties, good-looking, and full dues-paying members of the teen-age sub-culture. Both have long hair. They wear stylishly-cut animal hides. As Sonny sees them he jumps for his bow-slingshot.

8    ON SONNY – GROUP'S REVERSE ANGLE ▨▨▨▨▨▨

as he nocks an arrow, throws down on them.

> SONNY
> Beat it! Private property! No trespassing!

> BONAVENTURE
> (to Chér)
> Miss Ervine, reason with him!

(CONTINUED)

8       CONTINUED:

                          SONNY
                      (howling mad)
              She isn't Miss Ervine!  I married her!
              Her name is <u>Mrs.</u> Giacopetti, now scram!

9       CLOSE GROUP SHOT - FAVORING SAM & HONEY

Sam has had it.  His patience is ended, what with arrows
through the dashboard.  He starts forward.

                          SAM
                      (matter-of-fact)
              I'm gonna unpeel that kid like a banana.

Honey grabs him before he takes two steps.

                          HONEY
              Hold it, Sam.
                      (to Sonny, loud)
              Mr. Giacopetti...someone is trying to
              kill you.  You need protection.  These
              attorneys are friends of the Ervine
              family, they've hired us to--

10      ON SONNY
                          SONNY
              The Ervines?  Those nuts?  I need your
              help about as much as an extra set of
              elbows.

Suddenly Chér SCREAMS and a BOULDER CRASHES just beside Sonny.
CAMERA ANGLE EXPANDS as CAMERA PULLS BACK & UP.  We see a
man on the cliffs above, kicking down rocks to start an
avalanche.  Rocks and boulders plummet toward the two young
kids as the ASSASSIN works feverishly.

11      FULL SHOT - HONEY IN F.G.

as she pulls out her gun, steadies her hand and snaps off
a shot.  The bullet spangs off the rocks near the assassin
but misses him.  Sonny & Chér collide in their attempts
to get out of the way of the boulders.  Sonny falls out
of danger, but Chér slips as rocks cascade about her.
Honey fires again, and the assassin turns to flee.

12      CLOSEUP ON ASSASSIN

as his foot slips on the rocks, and he teeters, trying to
steady himself with a frantic bird-like waving of arms.
He falls backward with a long shriek.

13    SAME AS 11

as the assassin plunges to his death.  The rocks stop
falling.  The group moves in toward the crumpled figure
in the rock-pile.  Sonny & Chér come down from the ledge.
CAMERA MOVES IN till we are looking down at the dead man
who will tell no tales.

                    SONNY
                 (philosophical)
        You may be right.  We may need some
        help.

CAMERA HOLDS on Honey and Sam exchanging rueful looks as we:


                              FADE OUT:


            (COMMERCIAL INSERT)

## ACT I

FADE IN:

14    EXT. EDGE OF FOREST - DAY

as Limousine passes thru, on highway at edge of forest, we

FLASH MAINTITLES OVER

15    INT. REAR LIMOUSINE - DAY

CLOSEUP on map of Ervine Estate showing forest, house, cliffs and caves, highway. The map has been pulled down out of a map-case attached to the rear of the front seat.

> BONAVENTURE'S VOICE O.S.
> Ashford Ervine died little over a year
> ago. He left everything to Chér. The
> estate, the house, and what loose change
> he hadn't squandered.

As these previous remarks are made, Bonaventure's finger points out the location of the house at one end of the Estate, and the forest all the way to the opposite end.

CAMERA PULLS BACK to show Honey and Sam with Bonaventure between them, Belial and Contretemps in jump seats or in the front, one of them driving.

> HONEY
> Daddy was a spendthrift.

> BELIAL
> Women. They were his fatal weakness.

> SAM
> Filthy habit.

Honey gives him a look. One of <u>those</u> looks.

> CONTRETEMPS
> There was an inheritance, not a large
> one, but with the house it was sufficient.

> HONEY
> So these assassination attempts on
> Sonny, they couldn't just be a
> cover-up to get the girl?

(CONTINUED)

15     CONTINUED:

> BONAVENTURE
> Not a chance. There isn't enough
> money involved to risk murder,
> and certainly not enough to make
> it worthwhile hiring men like that
> --that--rock-thrower.

> BELIAL
> But there _was_ enough for Sonny to
> marry her!

> SAM
> Ah-ha! Venality rears its ugly head.
> The teen-age Tarzan is a fortune-
> hunter.

> CONTRETEMPS
> That's what the family contends.  But
> I don't agree with Bart.  If he was
> after her money, he wouldn't have
> done this caveman thing.

> BONAVENTURE
> (explains)
> The boy's a rebel.  Hates the Ervines
> and wants to prove he married the girl
> for love.  So they've renounced the
> world, he's proving they can live in a
> "primitive state".

> SAM
> Don't be too hard on him.  The kid's
> doing the best he can; he probably
> doesn't have a draft card to burn.

(CONTINUED:)

> HONEY
> What about the family?  Do they have
> a motive?  What about the house and
> estate?

> BELIAL
> She _gave_ them the house, signed it
> over for them to live in.  And the
> forestland, well, you've seen that...

> HONEY
> Mmm.  Yes, we've seen that.  So there
> isn't any reason for an attempt on
> her's life.  But why are they trying
> to kill Sonny?

(CONTINUED)

15   CONTINUED: - 2

                              HONEY
               What kind of a boy is he?  What did he
               do before he married the girl?

                              CONTRETEMPS
               Seems to be a right sort.  Nothing special.
               He worked at various jobs--lineman for the
               phone company, salesman, some office work
               for the gas company--never held any job
               for too long, sort of a knockabout.

                              HONEY
               What about the family?  Do they have a
               motive?  What about the house and estate?

                              BELIAL
               She gave them the house, signed it over
               for them to live in.  The oil is gone,
               so that's no consideration, what they
               call dead soil.  And the forestland, well,
               you've seen that...

                              HONEY
                          (examining ripped
                           hose)
               Mmm.  Yes, we've seen that.  So there
               isn't any reason for an attempt on
               Chér's life.  But why are they trying
               to kill Sonny?

                                        (CONTINUED:)

15    CONTINUED: - 13

                              CONTRETEMPS
              To be perfectly honest, we don't really
              care.  But as executors of the estate,
              it's our job to protect Chér, and as
              long as there's murder in the air around
              her...

                              BELIAL
              So that's your assignment.  Protect
              them.

                              HONEY
              But Sonny won't let us into their
              "primitive state".  So we'll have to
              work from the outside in.

16    FULL SHOT - EXT. ERVINE HOUSE - DAY (JUST AT DUSK, EERIE)

      as limousine pulls off highway, onto winding drive leading
      yonder to the mansion.  What a ghastly edifice. Gargoyles
      on the balustrades, dormers looking out ominously at them.

17    INT. LIMOUSINE - ANOTHER ANGLE

                              BONAVENTURE
              We're here.  Now you'll meet the
              Ervines.

                              HONEY
                         (confidently)
              There's something important in this we
              don't know, but I have an itchy feeling
              the Ervine family is the key.  We'll
              just check them out; Sam has a marvelous
              eye for spotting suspects.

      Car stops, they get out, approach front door.  As Sam
      pulls the old-fashioned door-chime, Honey HEARS a GRATING
      SOUND of stone against stone.  She looks up.

18    TILT-ANGLE - HONEY'S PERSPECTIVE OVERHEAD

      as a gigantic gargoyle teeters, obviously being pushed
      from behind where we can't see it.  It starts to fall.

                              HONEY
              Sam!  Move out!

      They each shove attorneys out of the way as CAMERA TILTS
      DOWN to catch action.  The gargoyle smashes with a roar
      where they were standing.  And then the door opens.

19    MED. CLOSE ANGLE ON DOOR - PAST HONEY

as it opens.  A very short, very strange looking little man
with wild hair and thick bottle-bottom glasses stands there.
It is COUSIN HARTSCHHORN ERVINE.

                    COUSIN HARTSCHHORN
          Serves you right.  No solicitors!

And he slams the door.  Honey and Sam exchange glances.
Rubble lies all about their feet.

                    BELIAL
          That was Cousin Hartschhorn.  You'd
          better try the bell again.

Sam edges back.

                    SAM
                   (cautious)
          No, I'll tell you what: <u>you</u> try the
          bell again.  I can't put <u>my</u> finger
          on it, but there's something kinda
          surly about the way they receive
          guests.

Honey is no less cautious, but she reaches out a hand, and
watching above, pulls the door-chime cord.  From within
is the COMIC CLANGOR of the chime, and the door opens.
An elderly woman with grey hair and wire-frame specs opens
it, and stands there smiling warmly at them.  She is
wearing a touch-football outfit.  It is GREAT-GRANNY OPAL.

                    GREAT-GRANNY OPAL
          Oh, lan'sakes and fret-my-whiskers, <u>do</u>
          come in.  You'll catch your death of
          the pip standing out there.

They troop in, all looking bewildered.

20    INT. FOYER - FULL SHOT

as Great-Granny Opal closes the door with the thud of a
crypt.  The foyer is high-ceilinged, very baroque and
rococco.

                    GREAT-GRANNY OPAL
                   (very sweet)
          I'm Great-Granny Opal.  Cousin
          Hartschhorn was very rude to speak
          to you that way.  He's being severely
          reprimanded for it.

At that instant a GHASTLY SHRIEK is heard from somewhere
in the bowels of the house.  Honey and Sam and the
Attorneys go rigid with horror, but Opal pays no heed.
                                        (CONTINUED)

20    CONTINUED:

> GREAT-GRANNY OPAL
> Won't you come on in, it's dinnertime.

She starts to lead them down the hall toward the living room as a small, pig-like child in football gear charges at her suddenly from a clothes closet. The little boy, AGNEW, tries to broken-field run around Granny's end, but the old lady sprints after him, tackles him and bears him to the floor.

> GREAT-GRANNY OPAL
> Sneaky, Agnew, very sneaky!  But I got you.  Fifteen yards penalty for hiding.  Back to the coal bin with you.

She gets up, drags him by the ear toward a basement stairway, and throws over her shoulder:

> GREAT-GRANNY OPAL
> (continues)
> Just go on in, and ask for Gracciella.

She vanishes down into the basement, slamming the door (which also clangs like a crypt, even though it's only wood). The group turns and enters the living room.

21    ESTABLISHING SHOT - LIVING ROOM - DAY

it is feeding time at the zoo.  A huge pot of some nameless steaming stuff is being ladled out by UNCLE YOGGOTH, a great hairy shambling yeti of a man, to a line of weirdies that winds snake-like through the room.  The ERVINE FAMILY.  A ghastly group of grotesque ghoulies and goblins guaranteed to grasp your gut and make you gulp and grunt.  Boy!  Are they ugly.  Tall ones, short ones, pinheads, caricatures. One looks like an English earl.  Another is dressed in WWI doughboy clothes.  Another wears a full-length evening gown.  There are farm types and city types and types you wouldn't believe.  They shuffle past the pot and take their slop.  Honey and Sam stare disbelieving.

> HONEY
> (stunned)
> Sam...has this good eye...for spotting ...suspects...

> SAM
> (equally stunned)
> The circus is in town...

22    ANOTHER ANGLE - UNCLE YOGGOTH IN ⬛ F.G.

looking gigantic, in his apron and with that great pot.
To the group approaching across the furniture-filled
living room with its chandeliers and junk bric-a-brac.
Honey and Sam reach him first.

                    HONEY
          Are you Gracciella?

                    UNCLE YOGGOTH
                (in a ridiculous falsetto
                 voice entirely wrong for
                 that great massive body)
          No, I'm Uncle Yoggoth.  Would you like
          some gruel?
                (he ladles a little)

                    SAM
                (looking ill)
          Gruel?  It looks like milk-fed tennis
          balls.

                    UNCLE YOGGOTH
                (affronted)
          Everyone's a gourmet!
                (beat)
          That's Gracciella over there.

He points to an exquisite girl on the opposite side of the
room, cleaning a double-barreled shotgun.  As they start
away from the line of diners, one old man who has been
slurping the glop from his bowl, suddenly clutches his
throat, shrieks and falls over.  Honey, Sam & Attnys
stare in horror as two other members of the clan drag the
body out of the room by the legs.

                    UNCLE YOGGOTH
                (furious)
          Everyone's a gourmet!

The group moves away, stunned and horrified.

23    CLOSE SHOT - ON GRACCIELLA

as the group approaches.  She looks up, sees them, gets
nasty look on her luscious face.

                    CONTRETEMPS
                (oily)
          Hello, Gracciella.

                    GRACCIELLA
          You lay one hand on me, Contretemps,
          and I'll jam this scattergun down
          your throat and use it for a pump
          handle!
                              (CONTINUED)

105

23    CONTINUED:

                         HONEY
            You've met before.

                         GRACCIELLA
            A dozen black-and-blue marks worth of
            howdy-do.  Stay away, Contretemps.

                         BONAVENTURE
            Miss Ervine--

                         GRACCIELLA
            Votrazenti.  I'm from the Milano
            branch of the family.

                         BONAVENTURE
            Miss Votrazenti, these are Miss Honey
            West and Mr. Sam Bolt; we've engaged
            them to watch out for Sonny & Cher...

Gracciella's eyes widen, her eyebrows go up, and she whips
out a police whistle.  She blows it LOUD.  The Ervine crowd
freezes.

                         GRACCIELLA
                         (announces)
            They're going to protect the heir and
            her husband!

There is a vicious murmur through the throng.  The crowd
has a definite lynch tenor.  Several nasty ones move
forward.

                         GRACCIELLA
                         (to Honey)
            You'd better get out of here while you
            can.  We don't care for those two.

                         HONEY
            But why?  They gave you this house!

                         GRACCIELLA
            Sure they did.  But Chér's father was
            the only one in this family with money,
            and so we all came here to collect, but
            he wasted it, all but a little of it,
            and so we all have to live here together
            till we can get the rest of the money,
            and there isn't enough to go around, so
            we spend all our time plotting to kill
            each other...

She swings suddenly and belts in the mouth with the barrel
of the shotgun a RELATIVE creeping up on her from behind
the sofa with a knife in his hand.  She goes on talking.

23    CONTINUED: - 2

                    SAM
          Which means all of you want Sonny
          and Chér down the tube.


                    GRACCIELLA
          What gave you your first clue, Tracy?


                    HONEY
          That makes all of you accessories to a
          conspiracy of murder.


                    GRACCIELLA
          Oh, wait a minute, that's not exactly
          true.  Not all of us want both of them
          dead.


                    SAM
          Ha-hah!  What'd I tell you, Honey, it's
          only Sonny they're after!  Okay, lady,
          where are the ones who want Sonny dead?


                    GRACCIELLA
          Third floor.  We've moved all the Sonny
          killers to the third floor.


                    HONEY
                    (stunned)
          The Sonny-killers?


                    GRACCIELLA
                    (matter-of-fact)
          Uh-huh.  Sonny-killers third floor;
          Chér-killers second floor; both-killers
          here on the main floor.


                    SAM
                    (quavery)
          Y'can't tell the players without a
          scorecard.


                    HONEY
          We may as well try the third floor.


                    GRACCIELLA
          You're hard to discourage.


                    HONEY
                    (sweetly)
          We need the work.


          She starts toward the front hall as the crowd parts for her.
          Gracciella stands to watch them go.  She is gigantic.  At
          least seven feet tall.  (Suggest BEA BRADLEY for this role.)

24    FULL SHOT - FRONT HALL - FAVORING STEEP STAIRCASE

as they start up, Honey in the lead, Sam following, the
three attorneys bringing up the rear.  As they get partway
up the stairs:

> HONEY
>
> Sam, I'll take the Sonny-killers on
> the ~~second~~ *third* floor, you take the Cher-
> killers on the second floor, and
> we'll--

This dialogue merely kills time as they reach the mid-point
in the flight of stairs.  At that time the stairs suddenly
go click! and the steps-and-risers go flat, making the
stairway a smooth slide, back down to the front hall.
As the stairs vanish, Honey and the rest scream and tumble
back down in a giant heap.

NOTE: timing is of utmost importance in this sequence!

A head appears at the top of the stairs with CAMERA SHOOTING
UP-ANGLE.  A weird head.  All hair.  There may be a face in
there, but all we see is a pair of bright, beady eyes, like
on a marmoset.  The Head cackles, and then begins reaching
behind to a bric-a-brac cabinet.

> THE HEAD
>
> Hard t'kill, you swine!  You're hard
> t'kill...

And he begins pelting them with bric-a-brac.  At that
moment huge, tall Gracciella emerges from the living room,
sees The Head and the group in a tumble, and unships the
scattergun.

> GRACCIELLA
> (to Head)
> No, you don't, Disraeli!  I saw them
> first, they're mine!

And she fires off both barrels, shattering the wall, and
sending The Head scampering.  Honey and her crew scuttle
on all fours toward the front door as the sounds of mayhem
rise higher and higher.  The crowd emerges from the
living room.

> GRACCIELLA
>
> Get 'em!

They try to get to the their feet, but they're too close
to the front door; on all fours they peddle for it, and
abruptly Granny Opal appears and opens it for them.  As
they race through she says sweetly:

                                        (CONTINUED:)

24    CONTINUED: - 2

                    GREAT-GRANNY OPAL
          Glad you could drop by; come again.

SHOT THRU DOOR as the group dashes away into the distance
and the SOUNDS of people murdering each other (crashes,
gunshots, gurgles, explosions, cars crashing, etc.) rises
on the air as we IRIS-FRAME IN on the tiny group running and

                              FAST IRIS CLOSE and

                              FAST IRIS OPEN on

25    EXT. HIGHWAY - AWAY FROM HOUSE - DAY

as limousine pulls into frame and stops.  Doors open and
everyone falls out, looking completely unhinged.  Sam leans
up against the car, the Attorneys cluster about trembling,
Honey slumps exhausted on a fender.

                    SAM
          This case may not be as easy as we
          thought.

                    BELIAL
          Monsters!  A houseload of monsters!

                    CONTRETEMPS
          We're lucky we escaped alive.

A GUNSHOT rings out and the bullet whaaangs past them.
They fall to the ground.

                    BONAVENTURE
          They're following us.

                    SAM
          Guerrilla warfare, they're stalking us
          through the woods.

                    HONEY
                 (calmly)
          I don't think they're the ones we're
          looking for.

                    BONAVENTURE
                 (to Heaven)
          There aren't enough suspects to suit
          her.

                    HONEY
          Who else would want Sonny dead?

                              (CONTINUED:)

25  CONTINUED:

Another SHOT goes careening overhead.  They ignore it.

                    CONTRETEMPS
          Well, there's always the gardener gardener,
          Mellors.

                    HONEY
          What's his part in this?

                    BELIAL
          Chér's father employed him.  He came
          from the Chatterley estate with
          excellent references.

                    BONAVENTURE
          But he was taken with Chér.  Made quite
          a play for her.  She rebuffed him when
          she met Sonny.  He was furious, made
          rather a shabby scene at the wedding, I
          hear.

                    HONEY
                    (to Sam)
          Sam, go find this the boy with the
          green thumb, and see how his garden
          grows.  I'm going back to guard Young
          America.

                    BELIAL
          Sonny won't let you in there unless
          you live as they do.  Can you?

                    HONEY
                    (grins)
          Apparently I never mentioned I come
          from a long line of pithecanthropus
          erectus's.

As Sam begins to slither away on his belly, into the
woods on the other side of the highway, another shot
SOUNDS and Honey concludes her last speech with a comic...

                    HONEY
                    (continues)
          Ooog, ooog, you Tarzan, me nauseous.

Sam throws her rueful glance and crawls away like an
infantryman as we

                              SMASH-PINWHEEL CUT TO:

26     EXT. GREENHOUSE - ERVINE ESTATE - DAY

EXT. CLOSEUP on nose stuck in flower.  CAMERA PULLS BACK
to show us a very Brendan Behan-type Welshman, wearing
high boots, breeches and full English squire gardening
gear.  He is a big number, all hair and muscles and looking
as though he tosses people around pubs for amusement.

                    SAM'S VOICE O.S.
          Is your name Mellors?

MELLORS looks up slowly from his flower.  He squints toward
CAMERA as Sam walks into frame from f.g.

                         MELLORS
                    (Welsh accent)
          Aye, that be m'name.  Mellors.  What
          be I c'n do fer'yuh?

27     ANOTHER ANGLE - 2-SHOT FAVORING MELLORS

He has a surly look, and leaning on his hoe, he looks like
he would as soon turn Sam into peat bog fertilizer as talk
to him.

                         SAM
          I'd like to ask you a few questions.

                         MELLORS
          Y'got a name, boy-o?  Er do they call
          y wit'a whistle?

                         SAM
          If I could understand what you were
          saying, I think I'd be insulted.

                         MELLORS
          A matter'u little moment.  What be
          yer title, son?

                         SAM
          Sam Bolt.  I'm working for the
          attorneys of Sonny and--

Before he can finish the sentence, Mellors howls like an
enraged bull and charges him with the hoe.  He swings the
hoe in a whistling arc, slicing a dozen blossoms from
their stems.

28     SHOT THRU GREENHOUSE TO ACTION

as they fight outside, we get a DISTORTED and CONCAVE
VIEW of the activity.  A battle royal, in which Sam
picks up a shovel and uses it like a quarterstaff as
he has a "pike fight" with Little John--er, Mellors.

29   CLOSEUP ON SAM

with the horizontal bar of the shovel cutting across his
face as the vertical bar of the hoe smashes across it,
in effect making a cross in center-screen.

30   MED. 2-SHOT - FROM XXX BELOW

SHOOTING UP BETWEEN the men as they circle one another,
like a pair of wary animals. Then Mellors leaps, and
swings and we hear an AUDIBLE WHIZZ as the hoe whips
across at Sam.

31
thru   SERIES OF HARD CUTS - ODD ANGLES
34
on the action. Let the CAMERA go wild!

35   SAME AS 28

as Sam swings that shovel like a baseball bat, catches
Mellors right across his Welsh kisser and sends him
flailing backward TOWARD CAMERA. Mellors crashes thru
the greenhouse glass, and lays LARGE IN F.G. on the
potting slab right up close to us. Sam comes TOWARD
CAMERA and grabs the semi-conscious Mellors, drags him out.

36   2-SHOT - IN CLOSE - LOW ANGLE

Mellors on his knees, Sam's face down close to Mellors'
face as he hangs onto Mellors shirt. Mellors looks a
good deal dopey and bloody. Sam is mussed.

                    SAM
       Now we talk?

                    MELLORS
       Y'have a way of makin' yer point.

                    SAM
       Okay. We talk.

He lets Mellors up. The gardener douses his face from a
watering can, and then slumps onto a bench outside the
greenhouse as Sam jacks a leg onto the bench and waits.

                    SAM
                 (continues)
       Why do you want Sonny Giacopetti
       dead?

                    MELLORS
       He took m'bird.

                    SAM
                 (repeats, dully)
       He took your bird.

                    MELLORS
       M'gurrul, m'Chér. He hoodwinked 'er.

37   ANOTHER ANGLE - ON SAM

                    SAM
          You're going to have to talk plainer
          than that.

                    MELLORS
          Aye, that was th'problum.  She always
          said that.  I'd haveta speak plainerrr.
          She said uh talkt like uh hadda mouthfulla
          peat moss.

                    SAM
          But you loved her.

                    MELLORS
          Like the very night wind that called her
          name.  Like the song of the earth beneath
          m'feet, the song that spoke her sweetness
          in tones of golden warmth; like the twerll
          of the grey babe birds against the dawn...
          like the...

He seems intent on going on, endlessly, sort of a cut-rate
Dylan Thomas.  Sam has to cut him off.

                    SAM
Yeah, sure.  The lyrics are great, but it hasn't got
          much of a beat...
                    (beat)
          let's get back to Sonny.

                    MELLORS
          He came along, after I'd woo'd 'er, after
          she'd come to like me...it was just a wee
          skip-hop till she'd've luved me.  But he
          spun 'er head with all that rebel
          nonsense, all that 'free spirit' hoot.
          He just wanted 'er money.  The rotter!

                    SAM
          So that's why you've been trying to kill
          him?

                    MELLORS
                    (affronted)
          Kill 'im?  Are y'daft?  I'd beat 'im
          senseless I would.  I'd punch his head
          t'putty, but I haven't tried t'do 'im in.

                    SAM
          There have been attempts on Sonny's life.
          So far yours is the healthiest motive.

                    (CONTINUED:)

37    CONTINUED:

Mellors rises, really insulted, and starts to move away.
Sam grabs him.

> SAM
> (continues)
> I always say: if it walks like a duck,
> quacks like a duck, smells like a duck
> and goes steady with ducks--chances are
> it's a duck...

> MELLORS
> (haughty)
> Is that whut'ya always say?

> SAM
> (cocky)
> That's what I always say.

> MELLORS
> (crushing)
> You must have some very ~~limited~~ dull
> conversations.

He walks away as Sam stares after and we HOLD for a beat
on his loss of face and then

> RAPID DISSOLVE TO:

38    EXT. FOREST - DAY

Foliage intrusive in f.g. as we SHOOT THRU it to a MED.
LONG SHOT on Sonny & Chér on their ledge.  We HEAR the
CRASH of foliage as someone comes o.s. toward the foliage
and the kids.  From that far distance we see Sonny hop
up, nock an arrow into his sling, and yell out across the
open space...

> SONNY
> Okay!  Don't come any closer!  Who
> is it?

SOUNDS come closer, louder.  Chér steps behind Sonny, he
moves to shield her.

> SONNY
> (menacingly)
> I'll put this arrow through you.  It'll
> go through three inches of plate steel,
> don't force me...!

CAMERA HOLDS thru foliage as a body comes from xtreme f.g.
and moves away from us in hard black and shadow, so we
cannot tell at first who it is.  Then Sonny (seen past body)
slowly lowers the sling, his face still menacing, but wary.

> (CONTINUED:)

38    CONTINUED:

                           SONNY
          Oh, it's you.

The visitor moves forward and now we can see who it is.
It is Honey, now barefoot, clad only in a fetching leopard-
skin.  It looks like something Dior might have whipped
up for Sheena, Queen of the jungle.  Honey poses, yeah!

                           HONEY
          I decided to slip into something
          comfortable.

She starts toward them.  CAMERA HOLDS as Honey moves away.

                           SONNY
                     (across open area)
          What's this all about?

                           HONEY
          You said I had to live on your level
          to guard you, so I made a quick stop
          at my friendly neighborhood dress
          shoppe.

                           CHÊR
                     (delighted)
          Oh, you look great, Miss West!

                           HONEY
          You should have seen the fight he put
          up.  Xxxx Pulling the skin off a
          leopard puts 'em in a real snit.

All of the foregoing dialogue runs over as Honey walks
toward them across the open area below the ledge.  But
when she first walks away, the CAMERA FAST UNFOCUSES and
as it FOCUSES BACK IN we see we are staring at Honey and
the kids thru a TELESCOPIC SIGHT.  The crosshairs move
left and right as Honey walks smoothly forward--as if
they were trying to center Sonny, but can't, because
Honey is in the way.  Finally, just as Honey moves left
a step, a RIFLE SHOT SOUNDS and as we HOLD THRU
TELESCOPIC SIGHT, we see Honey lurch forward, reach
up behind her own back in a terrible movement, and then
crash face-forward in the clearing.  Honey West is
dead, and no mistake about it, as we

ZOOM IN HARD thru the sight to XTREME CLOSEUP of corpse
lying absolutely motionless and then
                                        CUT TO BLACK
                                        and
                                        FADE OUT.

               (COMMERCIAL INSERT)

<u>ACT II</u>

FADE IN:

39    HIGH SHOT - BOOM CAMERA STRAIGHT DOWN - THE CLEARING - DAY

a FULL SHOT of the SCENE. Honey lying supine, obviously
dead. Sonny & Chér standing by, staring at her corpse.
And in a beat, Sam crashing through the edge of the forest
to stumble into the clearing. He sees Honey and takes a
stunned, hesitant footstep forward. Then two. Then another,
and finally kneels beside her dead body.

40    LOW ANGLE - HONEY LARGE IN F.G.

as Sam kneels above her, his face desolate. Sonny & Chér
in the UP-ANGLE beyond Sam. They lean in.

                    SONNY
          It was a rifle shot from over there.
          She's...dead.

                    CHÉR
          Dead. They killed her. She's dead.

                    SAM
                 (destroyed)
          She's dead...

                    HONEY
                 (suddenly)
          All right already, so I got the
          message. I'm dead. Another minute
          you'll be crying, and this leopard-
          skin isn't pre-shrunk.

Their faces register disbelief. Honey gets to her feet
as CAMERA RISES to follow her movements. They stare.
She half-turns as she speaks, and begins fumbling with
something under her leopard-skin.

                    HONEY
          I don't mind your <u>thinking</u> I'm stupid,
          but kindly don't <u>stare</u> at me like I'm
          stupid. Whaddaya think: if I was going
          to be running around out here with some
          screwball trying to de-foliate the
          population--

                              (Continued:)

40    CONTINUED:

Honey whirls around, holding a bullet-proof vest she has
been wearing under her leopard-skin.  It has a nasty hole
in the small of the back.  She holds it aloft like a
trophy as she concludes her speech.

                    HONEY
                 (triumphant)
          I wasn't gonna do it naked as a jaybird.

                    SAM
          Captain Fang rides again.

                    HONEY
          Whaddaya think, you're dealing with a
          starry-eyed kid?
                 (beat)
          So what else is new?

                    SAM
          Your number one suspect is Mellors, child
          of the soil.  When I mentioned Sonny, he
          tried to reupholster my face with a hoe.

                    HONEY
          Most amazing case of instant plastic
          surgery I've ever seen.

                    SAM
                 (sarcastic)
          I was able to subdue the ruffian.  And
          then we talked.
                 (to Sonny)
          He doesn't like you a lot.

                    CHÊR
                 (distressed)
          Oh, I know Mellors...he may be a bit
          fast-tempered, but he wouldn't try to
          kill Sonny.  He just doesn't know
          Sonny.

                    SAM
          Acquaintance makes very little difference
          to Mellors.  He didn't know me either, and
          he tried to plant me.

                    HONEY
          Any immediate danger from him?

                    SAM
          I don't think so.  He's obviously hired
          side-boys to do the actual work.  What
          snipers you get here are the only problem.

They both consider the hole in the bullet-proof vest.

41    ANGLE ON HONEY

as an idea comes to her.

                        HONEY
          Sam, what happened to the body of the
          man who fell off the cliff?

                        SAM
          DOA the cooler room downtown.

                        HONEY
          Get down there and find out who he was,
          what his background was.  Trace it thru,
          it might give us a lead.

Sam looks disturbed.  He takes Honey aside so the kids
can't hear.

42    TIGHT 2-SHOT - HONEY & SAM

                        SAM
                     (worried)
          Listen, these kooks are in real trouble.
          And he won't let us in here with any
          electronic gear, so how the devil am I
          going to get back in touch with you?

                        HONEY
                     (grins)
          The shoemaker's elves have been busy.

From the waistband of her leopardskin, Honey pulls out a
boomerang.  She flips up one end of it, and exposes a tiny
transistorized radio transmitter.  Sam smiles his admiration.
They return to Sonny & Chér.

                        HONEY
                     (to Sonny)
          Okay, we're all squared away, right?
          I can stay on with you.

                        SONNY
                     (reluctantly)
          I gave my word.

                        HONEY
          Chér, can you think of anyone else who
          might want Sonny out of the way?  For
          any reason whatever?

Chér considers a moment, then shakes her head no.

43    FULL SHOT - THE SCENE

                              HONEY
          Then until we have a beefier suspect,
          we'll stick with Mellors.  It may be
          hard to think of him as likely, but
          that's the way you'll have to think,
          so we can protect you two.

                              CHÉR
                          (reluctantly)
          Perhaps you're right.  There isn't
          enough money in my inheritance to make
          someone go this far--
                          (she waves a hand)
          --and the land is worthless...so what
          other reason could there be for someone
          to be after Sonny.

     As she mentions Sonny's name, Sam looks around, and sees
     Sonny has wandered away from the group, is standing off
     by himself, brooding.  We FOLLOW SAM'S POV and

                          CAMERA ZOOMS IN ON

44    SHOT - SAM'S POV

     to Sonny's left, at the verge of the forest, where a
     VICIOUS KILLER type is poised, about ready to hurl a
     wicked-looking WWI-style potato masher grenade.  The
     CAMERA ZOOMS IN on him and we HEAR SAM'S VOICE scream:

                          SAM'S VOICE O.S.
                              (warning!)
                Sonny!  Look out!

     CAMERA PULLS RAPIDLY BACK to fill the screen with the
     FULL SHOT again, as Sam hurls himself forward.  The
     potato masher is flung by the killer, spins end over
     end and hits right near Sonny.  Sam takes him out in a
     long, looping dive, and then he scrambles back, grabs
     up the grenade and hurls it as far as he can into a
     gulley.  The killer runs off into the forest.  There is
     no explosion.  Sam gets to his feet as other join him.

                              SAM
          That was a potato masher from the first
          World War.  Must be a dud.  We're only
          lucky whoever our killer is, he's hiring
          some of the most inept assassins on the
          market.

                              HONEY
          That must have been our sniper, taking
          another crack.  Sam...get moving.  Find
          out what you can about that guy at the
          morgue.
                                        (CONTINUED:)

44    CONTINUED:

                                    SAM
                    This is getting ridiculous!  The woods
                    are full of loonies; they'll try strafing
                    you with dive bombers next!

                                    HONEY
                    Go on, we'll be all right.  We'll go up
                    into the cave.

                                    SAM
                                  (reluctant)
                    Be careful.

                                    HONEY
                    Now that's gotta be the most useless
                    suggestion of the current social season.
                    You be careful: you might catch chillblains
                    at the morgue.

          Sam pulls a rueful face and stalks away, warily.  The
          kids and Honey start up into the cave as we

                                              DISSOLVE TO:

45    INT. CAVE - NIGHT

          CLOSEUP ON TV SET with a cartoon playing.  A cat is chasing
          a mouse, or a dog is chasing a chicken, or somesuch.  CAMERA
          PULLS BACK to show Chér sitting on the beaten earth floor,
          chewing on a chicken leg, absorbedly watching the cartoon.
          Behind her, Sonny is sharpening some arrows, as Honey sits
          looking bored.

                                    HONEY
                                  (to Sonny)
                    I thought you didn't want any modern
                    conveniences around?

                                    SONNY
                    Chér is having a little trouble getting
                    acclimated to the natural life.  I figured
                    it would be easier to break her in a
                    little bit at a time.

                                    HONEY
                                  (absently)
                    Talk about long extension cords...

                                    SONNY
                                  (suddenly)
                    I bet you think I'm some kind of post-teen
                    age nut or something, don't you?

                                              (CONTINUED:)

45    CONTINUED:

> HONEY
> (mock shocked; delivers
> line like W.C. Fields)
> Why in the world would I think that someone
> who goes to live in a cave and wear animal
> hides in the middle of the 20th Century is
> a nut?  Don't be ridiculous.

46    CLOSE SHOT - SONNY (INTERCUT WITH HONEY)

He puts down the arrows and gets very defensive in explaining.

> SONNY
> Listen, let me tell you something: out
> there I'm just a dust-collector; I pick up
> my measly paycheck and scuff along hopin'
> something'll break for me, right?  So if
> I'm a real good boy maybe they won't grab
> me and ship me off to some half-pint war
> on the other side of noplace, and maybe
> I'll make it to sixty-something and get
> my peanut money so I can grow old in
> genteel poverty.  So you tell me: which
> makes more sense, living like a human
> being on my own, out here, with my hands,
> making it like I can...or choking to death
> in some walkup flea-trap?

> HONEY
> If you can set that to music, you've got
> a fine protest song.

> SONNY
> (disgusted)
> Ahhh, you conformists!  You're all alike.

Honey does a take.  Her take includes everything offbeat
about her we know from past shows, and the fact that she
is about as non-conformist as they come.  Also, that she
is wearing a leopard-skin, crouched down with him in
this cave.  He is obviously a disgruntled rebel.

> HONEY
> (escaping)
> Philosophy is too deep for me.  Do you
> have anything around here to pass the
> time while we're waiting to be murdered?

> SONNY
> (indicating shelf
> in rock wall)
> There's some books in there.

47   TRUCKING SHOT - CLOSE WITH HONEY

as she goes to the shelf, and pulls out half a dozen paper-
backs, some comics, a cook book and then...she sees something
far in back, and fishes it out.  She holds it up and we can
read the title on the pamphlet over her shoulder.  She reads
it <u>softly</u>, aloud, as CAMERA HOLDS ON TITLE:

                    HONEY
                    (s.v.)
        "RE-CYCLING PROCESSES IN THE STORAGE
        OF NATURAL GASES FOR DEPLETED OIL FIELDS"

She looks confused, shakes her head and puts it back where
it came from, selecting a comic book instead.  We see the
comic over her shoulder:

                    HONEY
                    (s.v.)
        Hawkman and the Fanged Fossils of Fear.
        Much better.

She takes the comic and moves into the light of the wood
fire burning in its shallow pit, as Chér continues to
watch the animals chew on each other, and Sonny sharpens
his weapons.  She settles down to read when...

48   FULL SHOT THRU CAVE MOUTH - NIGHT

there is a helluva SHRIEK from the forest.  They all leap
up.  Honey grabs her boomerang, Sonny grabs his sling,
and Chér grabs Sonny.

                    CHÉR
                    (terrified)
        Whu-what was that...?

                    HONEY
        The call of the wild.

                    SONNY
                    (triumpahant)
        Someone's caught in one of my traps.

Honey gives him a look.  Daniel Boone.  They start out of
the cave, cautiously.  The SHRIEK comes again.

49   REVERSE ANGLE - ON THE GROUP

as they leave the ledge, cross the clearing and enter the
woods.

50   TRUCKING SHOT - WITH GROUP

as they move through forest toward the THIRD SHRIEK.

51    HIGH-ANGLE FULL SHOT - THE FOREST - NIGHT (suggest day for night)

CAMERA ANGLED DOWN toward the group as they mush their
way into a small clearing.  ROPE VERTICALLY BISECTS frame,
in XTREME F.G. and as CAMERA COMES DOWN holding on the
group as they come toward us, we travel down the rope as
well, till we encounter a noose, a naked foot caught in
the noose, and then a naked leg, x followed immediately
by Gracciella Votrazenti, hanging upside-down, about four
feet off the ground.  HOLD Gracciella's head in f.g. as
the forest wanderers come up to her.  She is struggling
mightily, and trying to get loose.  Sonny bends down and
picks up the shotgun she has dropped.

                    SONNY
You dropped something, on your way up.

                    GRACCIELLA
I am not happy.

                    CHÉR
Life can be very difficult sometimes.

                    GRACCIELLA
If I hang like this much longer, I will
be sick all over you.

                    SONNY
See that, Miss West.  Right here in our
own front yard, threats and personal
vilification.

                    HONEY
                (to Gracciella)
It's probably poor taste to ask this,
but whyfor are you skulking about
here in the forest primeval so late
at night.

                    CHÉR
She's the sniper!  There's her rifle.

                    GRACCIELLA
I am not!  Rifles are for sneaks.  I
was coming over to blow your heads
off with my shotgun.

                    HONEY
                (reluctantly)
Heaven knows I'd like to believe she's
our patsy, but she's probably telling
the truth.  That's a scattergun, Chér.
Whoever shot at me used a rifle; so
unless she's packing a concealed weapon
            (Honey scrutinizes tight
             clothing on Gracciella)
the sniper's still out here somewhere.

52    PAST GROUP IN 3-SHOT TO GRACCIELLA

                    GRACCIELLA
        If you really want to know who's behind
        all this, I'll tell you, only let me
        down!

                    SONNY
        You'll stay up there; I've got a good
        mind to put an arrow through you.

He starts to nock an arrow as Honey grabs him.

                    HONEY
        Hold it, Fearless.
                    (to her)
        You know who's behind this?

                    GRACCIELLA
        Sure!  Everyone at the house knows.
        It's--

Her words are interrupted by a RIFLE SHOT that rings out
and then another.  Honey and the kids fall flat as the
rope is severed and Gracciella falls on her head.  Honey
sees movement in the trees and unlimbers her boomerang.
She flings it and it hits a tree, falls.  Sonny lets fly
an arrow and the sniper crashes away and is lost in the
woods.  They pay attention to Gracciella.

                    CHÉR
        She's dead.

                    SONNY
        Yeah, she's dead.

                    HONEY
        I've been in this elevator before.
                    (beat)
        She's not dead, just knocked silly.
        The bullet severed the rope.  If he
        hadn't been aiming for her, that'd
        be pretty fine shooting.

Gracciella groans, sits up.

                    GRACCIELLA
        --the killer is one of the Attorneys.

                    HONEY
        Now I know why they say women always
        have the last word.

                              (CONTINUED:)

52    CONTINUED:

                              GRACCIELLA
              My head hurts.  Oooo, what a headache!

                              HONEY
              You'll have to wait your turn, I've had
              ~~mx~~ mine longer.
                              (beat)
              Now how do you know it was one of the
              Attorneys?

                              GRACCIELLA
              Because we almost caught him in the attic
              with the trunk.

                              HONEY
              I knew it sounded too simple.  What attic?
              What trunk?

                              GRACCIELLA
              The one with the papers in it, in our
              house.

                              HONEY
                              (looks relieved)
              Oh, <u>that</u> trunk.

         She goes to retrieve her boomerang.

53    CLOSEUP ON HONEY

         as she flips up the end of the boomerang, and sees the
         transmitter is shattered into little pieces.

                              HONEY
              Shows the horrors of unskilled labor.

54    FULL SHOT

         as Honey returns to the group.

                              HONEY
                              (to Gracciella)
              ~~Namxxexxxxxx~~ Would you believe I don't
              know what trunk you're talking about?

                              GRACCIELLA
              No.

                              HONEY
              Would you believe I have a <u>small</u> idea?

                              GRACCIELLA
              No.
                                          (CONTINUED)

54    CONTINUED:

We suddenly realize they are doing a Don Adams bit.

                    HONEY
            Well, then, you'd better believe
            we're going up to that attic.

                    GRACCIELLA
            That, I'll believe.

She helps Gracciella up.  The girl towers over Honey, but
Honey is brandishing that boomerang.  Honey turns to the
kids.

                    HONEY
            You two get back to the cave, and stay
            there.  Jack the Ripper is still prowling.

They turn to go as Honey moves off a step with Gracciella.

                    HONEY
            And as for you, little sister, how
            are you fixed for face powder?

                    GRACCIELLA
            Huh?

                                SPIN-FRAME TO:

55    INT. ATTIC - NIGHT

CLOSE ON TRUNK LID as face powder sifts down from above.
CAMERA PULLS BACK to show Honey dusting the lid of the
trunk with face powder as Gracciella holds a candle.

                    GRACCIELLA
            How's that going to help?

                    HONEY
            An ancient and mystic art I picked up
            in the jungles of Yucatan.  It's called
            dusting for latent fingerprints.

The prints do come up.  Honey gives a gasp of pleasure.

                    HONEY
            Now all I have to do is photograph them
            and run them through the files.

                    GRACCIELLA
            You don't have a camera.

Honey removes an earring, presses a stud, and out comes
a lens.  Miniature camera.  She clicks off a few.

                                (CONTINUED:)

55    CONTINUED:

                              GRACCIELLA
                             (naturally)
          Mine only hang from my ears.

                              HONEY
          Why were all your relatives lurking
          on the stairs when we came up?

                              GRACCIELLA
          They were waiting for the Attorney
          to come back.

                              HONEY
                             (lifts trunk lid)
          Now what exactly is in here he wanted?

                              GRACCIELLA
          Papers for dummy corporations Chér's
          father owned.  About two and a half
          million dollars worth of assets under
          three or four phoney names.

                              HONEY
                             (reasoning)
          So one of the Attorneys knew about the
          deals, and came for the papers.  Why
          didn't he get them?

                              GRACCIELLA
          We caught him sneaking up here.  My
          relatives chased him.  He went out
          that window there.

     She points to a broken dormer window, facing out on some
     trees.  We can see a trellice.

                              HONEY
          So you and the folks have been waiting
          for him to make another grab.

                              GRACCIELLA
          And I was going out to get rid of the
          heir, so we could inherit these
          corporations.

                              HONEY
          I'll have to get these photos down to the
          lab.  Then we'll know who our killer is.

     We HEAR a HEAVY CREAKING and past them we see a section
     of wall against which crates and old boxes and antiques
     have been stacked, slowly opening.  Whee!  A secret panel.

56    REVERSE ANGLE - ATTORNEYS POV

SHOOT THRU SECRET PANEL as Belial, Bonaventure and
Contretemps step into room.  Past them to Honey and the
giant Gracciella.  All three carry guns.

                    BONAVENTURE
          You're no fun at all, Miss West.  You
          were supposed to be romping through the
          woods with the Bobbsey Twins while we
          took the papers.

                    BELIAL
          You would have made a fine alibi for us
          later.  But now we have to cancel your
          policy.

                    HONEY
          So it was you three.  All in it together.
          Kill Sonny, and then Chér as bereaved widow
          turns all the legal work over to you, and
          you smoothly alter the names of the dummy
          firms and cop the goodies.

                    CONTRETEMPS
          We had nothing to do with those assassination
          attempts.  We don't know who did.  That's
          why we called you in.  If you found the
          right suspect, when we killed them, all
          suspicion would gxxxxxgxxxxxx be directed
          to the one you'd uncovered.

                    BELIAL
          Long explanations bore me.  Let's do it.

Honey suddenly slaps sidewise at the candle Gracciella
holds.  The attic is plunged into darkness.  In the darkness
we SEE GUNFLASHES, we HEAR PUNCHES and GRUNTS OF PAIN.
We SEE a body being flung against a wall.  We HEAR a
SHRIEK from a woman.  This goes on for several beats.
Then we see a swaying light coming through a door in the
rear of the attic it is a lantern being carried by Great-
Granny Opal.  She comes in, the room is filled with light
and we see that Honey and Gracciella have knocked the
three Attorneys silly.  They lie in an untidy heap.

                    GREAT-GRANNY OPAL
          Shoulda let me know, sweetheart, I'd
          have fixed the guest rooms.

                    HONEY
                 (suddenly shocked)
          Wait a minute!  If these three
          haven't made any attempts on Sonny,
          than and you Ervines haven't gotten
          to them, them that only leaves one
          suspect!  And I left those kids out
          there alone!

57
thru AERIFLEX SHOTS - WITH HONEY
60

as she rushes out of the attic, down a flight of stairs, out the front door of the Ervine house, through some woods and into a clearing in which Sam Bolt (running from the other direction) collides with her. They both fall down.

61　2-SHOT

as they sit there staring dumbly at each other. Then Honey's frantic air prevails and she yells.

> HONEY
> Mellors! It has to be Mellors!

> SAM
> Wait a minute...I tried to reach you
> from the morgue but your transmitter
> didn't answer...

Honey climbs to her feet, pulls Sam up.

> HONEY
> No time to talk! Mellors is the
> killer. And I left Sonny & Chér
> alone out there. Come on!

They dash off together.

62　AERIFLEX CLOSE PAN WITH THEM

as they run. Sam yells to her as they dash thru woods.

> SAM
> Th-that guy who fuh-fell off the
> cliff. He was just a guy, nobody
> special...worked for the gas
> company...hired out once in a
> while to bash people...

They rush forward and break into the clearing as we see:

63　FULL SHOT

the cliff and environs. Mellors is stalking across the open space toward Sonny & Chér. Sam rushes for Mellors but this time the Welshman knocks him aside. In the same moment, however, Honey dashes for the kids. As she nears them, she suddenly stops, and turns to CAMERA that has been following close. She says, to herself, as though the light has just dawned, but INTO CAMERA:

> HONEY
> The gas company?

64     ANOTHER ANGLE - PAST SONNY & CHÉR

to Honey, as a RIFLE SHOT rings out, Honey dives across the
short space intervening, and instead of pulling Sonny
down, she grabs Chér.  The bullet shatters rock precisely
where Chér was standing.  Then Honey yells to Sam.

                    HONEY
                    (loud)
          Sam!  He's at the edge of the
          woods!  Get him!

And as Sam takes off after the sniper, leaving Mellors
standing confused, Honey gets to her feet.

                    SONNY
          Are you gonna protect me from that
          killer?
                    (he points at Mellors)

                    HONEY
          I sure am, pussycat.

And she hauls off with a roundhouse that lifts Sonny off
his feet and sends him flat-out against the cave wall.
He slides down and settles silently with a dumb smile on
his face.  Chér screams.

                    CHÉR
          Miss West, that was my husband.
          You weren't supposed to hit <u>him</u>!

                    HONEY
          If Sam brings that sniper back, and
          that sniper works for the gas company,
          then yours was a marriage that was
          definitely <u>not</u> made in Heaven.

CAMERA HOLDS on Chér's woebegone face as she stares down
at the unconscious Sonny and we
                              DISSOLVE TO:

65     INT. JAIL - CELL BLOCK - DAY

the cells are filled.  Reading from left to right: Belial,
Bonaventure and Contretemps; Gracciella and assorted
Ervine relatives; Mellors; Sonny.  On the outside, walking
down the line, come Sam and Honey and Chér.

                    HONEY
                    (explaining)
          Sonny worked at the gas company long
          enough to find out they were desperate
          for land they could use for storing
          natural gas.  He found out that in many
          cases where this has been done on land
          containing depleted oil wells, the
                    (MORE)
                              (CONTINUED:)

65    CONTINUED:

                              HONEY (CONT'D.)
          restored gas pressure reactivated the
          wells.  The estimate on your land is
          120 barrels a day.  It's called the
          re-cycling process.

                              CHÉR
          He never told me...

                              HONEY
          You should have checked his reading
          habits.  When a guy like Sonny puts
          down "Hawkman and the Fanged Fossils
          of Fear", and starts reading geology
          pamphlets, there's something wrong,

                              SAM
          He hired two bums who worked with him
          to make phoney attempts on his life,
          knowing Mellors would be suspected,
          and when the final attempt on him
          just happened to misfire and get you--

                              CHÉR
          He'd inherit my land and sell it to
          the gas company.

                              HONEY
          What he didn't know was that there
          was another plot going...by the Three
          Musketeers here...to get all the dummy
          assets your father had hidden.

                              SAM
          And your family was about ready to go
          get you.

                              CHÉR
          If I didn't know better, I'd think
          people were out to hurt me.

                              HONEY
          You're just paranoid.

                              SAM
          But...a wealthy paranoid.

                              CHÉR
          But I don't understand why Mellors was
          coming to get Sonny.

                              HONEY
          He was just bugged at Sam's accusing
          him of plotting murder.

66    CLOSER SHOT - MELLORS IN MID-B.G.

                        CHÉR
            So why is he here in jail with
            everyone else?

                        HONEY
            Well, Sam had him booked for assault
            with a deadly weapon, but actually it's
            because we don't like to tell the
            solution too many times, it gets tiring.

        CAMERA HOLDS on Sam's outraged expression as Chér manages
        to work up a tiny smile; then, staring at Sonny, she bursts
        into tears, and as Honey gives her a hankie we:

                                        FADE OUT:


                (COMMERCIAL INSERT)



                        THE END

You Can't Get There from Here

## Editor's Note: No Sally in His Alley

"How I came to do *The Flying Nun* is inordinately discursive and oblong," recalls Ellison, explaining a brief business liaison with a manager that evaporated when Ellison decided shoe leather was a better recipe for getting work than a high-priced go-between. Nevertheless, the ex-manager did open one door of interest to the writer.

"I had been following Sally Field in a purely adolescent, gob-smacked way since her days on *Gidget*. I had no idea what an incredible actress she was. All I knew was that I thought she was what they'd now call 'very hot.' I desperately wanted to hook up with Sally Field."

Impressed by the supporting cast and in lust with the lead, Ellison was under no delusions as to the quality of the vehicle, "an incredibly silly series based on a book about a nun whose wimple looked like a seagull, and she was so small and so fragile—and her bones were apparently those of a bird: hollow—that in a strong wind, she could fly; thus, *The Flying Nun*." Likening his writing assignment on the series to the perversity of Leopold Sacher-Masoch being employed to write a *Bobbsey Twins* book, Ellison pitched, was hired, wrote, and submitted his script to Screen Gems who paid him... and heard nothing further.

Some time later, he received a phone call from Irma and Rocky Kalish, a well-respected wife-and-husband writing team. "Irma called me and said, 'We're doing a re-write on a script of yours.' She said it with uneasiness. I said, 'What script?' She said, 'It's a *Flying Nun*.' I said, 'What's the problem with it?' Irma said, 'Let me put Rocky on...' I thought to myself can it be *that* bad? Rocky came on, laughing: 'Well, the network rejected it because its too Jewish.' *Too Jewish?! It's about a nun!*

"Rocky said, 'Let me read you a couple lines...' He read me a couple lines where Sister Bertrille meets the girlfriend of Alejandro Rey's character. The girl says, 'I'm such and such,' then Sister Bertrille—a Catholic nun—says... Well, you'll read the line."

"You Can't Get There from Here," closed *The Flying Nun*'s first season on ABC (Samish had moved on to Quinn Martin Productions by this time, and if you don't know about him, you should have bought BRAIN MOVIES, Volume 2!) on 11 April 1968. It was credited to Cordwainer Bird, likely due to the cost-cutting flashbacks to earlier episodes added by the Kalishes.

"Long career, lot of strange jobs," says Ellison. "A lot of them I did to make a buck; this one I did to get laid—a complete and total failure. I don't know which is nobler: doing a job for money (and they say you're just a whore), or doing a job to gain a woman's favor (by which you're trying to get sex by doing art). It's an interesting debate."

THE FLYING NUN

segment: YOU CAN'T GET THERE FROM HERE

written by HARLAN ELLISON

TEASER:

Sister Bertrille, overcome with the joys of a summer day,
has given in to the wanderlust that assails all young girls
when the sunshine season hits its most idyllic.  She is
out over the ocean, doing your basic rolls, dives and
Immelmanns (and making sounds that are suspiciously like the
sounds of a Spandau machine gun); and once we hear her
murmur under her breath, "Take that, Red Baron!  And nuts
to the Kaiser, too!"

Abruptly, the thermal updrafts fail, she hits a calm
place in the sky, and begins to drop.  She manages to
aim herself at a tiny island down there, and glides all but

the last thirty feet, at which point the wind fails completely,
and she tumbles coronet over cassock into a stand of prickly
pear (or its desert island equivalent). Her coronet, yanked
off her head at the last moment of impact has been ripped
by a tree, and fallen in the water.

Sister Bertrille pulls herself out of the underbrush,
and delicately tries to pull the underbrush out of <u>her</u>.
Then she takes stock, determines nothing is broken, and
seeks her coronet. It is lying at the edge of the beach,
washing in and out with the lapping of the waves. She picks
it up, and it is a bedraggled, ripped mass of soggy cloth.
Her flying is over, at least for the time being.

In pantomime, she begins to assay her situation, decides
she will just have to do something about it, and starts
by cupping her hands and yelling if anyone is there. No
answer. She shrugs. I'm alone.

She quickly fashions something like a clothesline and
hangs the coronet up to dry. Then she gathers some little
sticks, and some tinder and tries to get a fire going.
It doesn't work. She will have to find something that
burns better. She starts up the beach.

Suddenly, she sees a footprint. Of a bare foot.

The voice of Sister Jacqueline informs us that Sister
Bertrille's first thought is: <u>Do the natives still make
hero sandwiches out of missionaries</u>? And if so, <u>are the
natives restless tonight</u>?                    FADE OUT.

ELLISON / 3

ACT ONE:

Sister Bertrille follows the trail of bare footprints,
and finds, sitting at the edge of the beach, throwing small
rocks into the water, and looking disconsolate, CARLOS
RAMIREZ. He is not happy.

She startles him and he gives a jump. When he sees who
it is, he looks as though all the Furies had assailed him
en masse. "No, it can't be," he moans. "Some men get washed
up on desert islands with Brigitte Bardot; some men get
cast adrift with Vanessa Redgrave; some men are castaway
even with perhaps Phyllis Diller and they can't complain.
Me...I get you! Always you! Everywhere I go! Are you
haunting me, Sister? Have you made it your mission in life
to make me an unhappy man?"

"You're raving," she answers.

"I'm unhappy," he replies.

She sits down beside him and in silence they throw rocks
for a few minutes. Suddenly they both get inspirations,
and turn to each other, speaking at once. When they sort
themselves out, Carlos asks:

"Where is your coronet? You can fly out for help."

"It got torn. I can't fly."

Then she asks, "We can take your yacht. We're saved."

Carlos shakes his head. "Wrong."

"Wrong?"

"Wrong."

ELLISON / 4

"Why?"

"I've been marooned."

Sister Bertrille is amazed. "By a mutinous crew of cutthroats?" she asks breathlessly.

He shakes his head. "By Estella Ruiz."

"She cast you adrift?"

"She threw me overboard."

"She was bigger than you."

"She moved faster than me."

Carlos relates, very briefly, how he lured the gorgeous blonde Estella on board the yacht, set sail for this remote island off the shipping lanes, with, uh, circumspect motives (at which Bertrille naturally frowns and tsk-tsks), and when they arrived, and he tried to make his pitch, she belted him, pushed him overboard, and split with the yacht.

"Well, we've got to make do the best we can," says Bertrille. "Survival is the important thing. Here we are, two lonely castaways on a terror-filled island in the empty ocean. It'll be tooth and nail if we expect to live out the years till a chance merchantman stumbles upon us here."

Carlos looks at her as though she's insane. "What're you talking about? As soon as Estella feels remorseful enough, she'll turn around and come back. I'm going to sit here and wait for her."

Thus begins the first argument between the castaways.

ELLISON / 5

Carlos intends to sit right there, not expend unnecessary energy, merely indulge his anger at the girl who absconded with his yacht. Bertrille insists they make preparations for a long stay, a la Robinson Crusoe. Wild beasts. Exposure. The rigors of the night. Starvation. Dying of thirst. Beri-beri. Rindapest. Hoof-and-mouth disease. An unexpected monsoon.

"Monsoons don't occur in these latitudes," Carlos points out.

"See! See how _unexpected_ it would be!" carols Bartrille.

Carlos throws up his hands, and decides the easiest thing to do is cooperate with the nut nun, and keep occupied till the yacht returns.

The first thing, Bertrille decides, is to get a big signal fire going. They have to gather firewood. She suggests he go one way, she'll go the other, and gather up as much as they can. He cannot understand why he is letting her boss him around, but he goes.

WIPE TO their return. Carlos staggering under an ungainly load of sticks and tree refuse...not carrying very much, and dropping most of what he has. From the other direction comes Bertrille, dragging behind her a kind of rough sledge made of sticks bound together by vines, and being pulled by a vine rope. It is loaded to the top with a small mountain of fodder for the fire. Carlos snarls.

Then Bertrille says they need something with which to
light the fire. Carlos pulls out his solid gold embossed
diamond-encrusted lighter. Bertrille takes a look at it,
and tosses the case away, keeping only the flint and
steel. Carlos shrieks. "That lighter was given to me by
the Marquessa of Moldavia, it's worth a fortune!"

Very dramatically, very Humphrey Bogart, Bertrille
waves away his complaint and says with castaway-hardened
tones, "Of what use is gold to us here? Of what use are
diamonds? It's survival now! Tooth and nail against the--"

"I know, I know!" Carlos yells.

Bertrille shrugs. "I was only trying to impress upon
you the seriousness of our plight."

Then she starts trying to ignite some tinder with the
flint and steel. It won't take. She needs something else.
She makes Carlos empty his pockets. She finds what she
needs to get the fire going. What is it? Naturally:

Money.

Carlos howls as she burns up two hundred dollars to
get her stupid signal fire going.

Next, they need something to eat. Bertrille takes a
safety pin from her habit, and bends it into a fish-hook.
She uses a vine and a stick for fishing, and tells Carlos
to dig worms. Dig worms!?! Of course dig worms, what do
you think fish eat? Barbecue beef sandwiches?

Carlos refuses to dig worms. It is demeaning. Beneath the station of a gentleman of Puerto Rico. And besides, it will ruin a perfectly good five dollar manicure.

Bertrille badgers him into going for worms. He stalks off, and Bertrille lets the line dangle in the water off a rock. In a second she has a bite, and pulls up a large fish.

She runs to tell Carlos she won't need worms, and can't find him. RAPID DISSOLVES THRU series of trucking shots of Bertrille racing madly through the underbrush, trying to find him.

Finally, she is standing at the edge of a glade, yelling, "Mr. Ramirez! Mr. Ramirez, where are you?"

A quiet voice from nearby says, very gently, "Over here, Sister."

She looks all around, cannot find him. "Where are you?"

"Here."

"Where?"

"Down here."

She looks a few feet away, at the ground. Carlos is up to his chest in quicksand.

She panics, does a typical Bertrille double-take, runaround and howl, very much like a Chinese fire & boat drill. Finally, Carlos suggests she tie a vine around a tree and throw him the end.

Later, they are sitting around the fire, Carlos'

clothes drying on his back. They are eating the fried fish after Bertrille says grace and thanks God for the bounty of the sea, and making them so comfortable under harrowing conditions. Carlos is <u>really</u> unhappy now.

Bertrille says it is his own fault for trying to take advantage of the girl on the yacht. They get into a conversation on Carlos' social attitudes, in which some snide (and it is to be hoped humorous) observations are made on the contemporary mating ritual.

But out of this conversation Bertrille begins to get the message that this Estella is not as nice and sweet a girl as she thought. Carlos talks about Estella, but the way he paints her, Bertrille begins to suspect she was on the grab herself.

Bertrille opines Carlos may not understand women as well as he thinks he does. Carlos refuses to listen to this. You can make him dig worms, burn his money, bury him in quicksand, but kindly do not shatter his self-image as a roué and conqueror of inscrutable femininity.

Sister Bertrille says their next problem is to build sleeping conveniences for the night.

Carlos says he does not intend to sleep there for the night. Bertrille says okay, if you don't want to help. She builds a little hammock in a tree. Carlos sulks.

Then she says they need fresh drinking water. She

suggests he go one way, she will go the other, around the
island, looking for where the foliage is greenest.  There
they should find fresh water.  Reluctantly--mostly because
he is thirsty--Carlos agrees.  He goes off one way, Bertrille
the other, with Carlos saying the yacht will return any moment.

As she passes a small rocky inlet, with the water
rushing in and out, Bertrille sees a frightening thing...

A hideous seaweed and fungus covered creature is
dragging itself out of the water behind the rocks.  She
screams starts to run, slips, falls, and is certain The
Creature From The Black Lagoon will devour her.

Then the Creature parts the seaweed, and it is a
blonde girl in a bikini.

"Who're you?" asks the Creature.

"Sister Bertrille, from the Convent of San Tancé.  Who
are you?"

"I'm Estella."

"Wheeew," breathes Bertrille.  "I thought sure you
were going to make a Bertrilleburger out of me..." and then
her mouth drops open in horror.  "Estella?"

The girl nods.

"From the yacht Estella?"

Again the girl nods.

"Hurray!  We're saved!" carols Bertrille, rising.
"Where is it, how soon can we leave?"

ELLISON / 10

"As soon as we can get to your boat," says Estella.

"My boat?" Bertrille asks querulously. "I thought we'd use _your_ boat."

"That would be difficult," says Estella.

"Don't say it," Bertrille winces and slaps hands over ears.

"I sank it," Estella says.

Bertrille looks sick. "I asked you not to say it."

                                        FADE OUT.


ACT TWO:

The VOICE of SISTER JACQUELINE O.S. tells us that Bertrille has given it much thought, and has decided it is best to keep Carlos and Estella unaware of each other's presence on the island.

So she has two separate communities of survival going, one on either side of the island.

We play between them, with Bertrille helping Estella get settled, and keeping Carlos out of trouble.

On the one hand, the girls erect a fairly decent little lean-to, and make themselves comfortable. FLIP to Bertrille in her attentive visit to Carlos. He has decided he doesn't need her help, and to prove it, he is going to make an S.O.S. in the sand, for passing planes to see. We come in on him running back and forth

from the edge of the water, getting his feet wet so when he
drags them through the dry sand in an S.O.S. shape, they
will make visible tracks. Bertrille stands with hands
folded, watching him rush frantically past her, back and
forth like a nut. Finally, exhausted, he stops before
her, panting, and says, triumphantly, "For a man of
indomitable will, there is always a way out! Skill and
cunning instinct will always win the day."

"You haven't had much experience at it, have you?"

Reluctantly, Carlos admits, "No, not much, but so
what?"

Bertrille points.

"You misspelled it."

She walks away.

Carlos looks. S.S.O.

FLIP.

Bertrille and Estella. The Sister has decided the
surest way for them to get off the island is for her to
try and repair the coronet. She makes up a bit of a story
for Estella (not really a white lie) that the reason
she wants to make starch out there on the island, and
sew up the ripped coronet, and patch it with a piece of
her habit, is that she doesn't feel "quite right" being out
of uniform. Estella buys it, and they set about making
starch in a cocoanut pot, while Bertrille improves a

needle from a kind of island fir (or whatever it is they
have of that specie on islands) and by unraveling several
pieces of cloth from her habit.

FLIP.

Bertrille comes upon Carlos. He is stripped down to
his bathing suit, rubbing some kind of sticky substance
on his chest and back.

"What're you doing?"

"I'm greasing myself down for a long swim."

"Where to?"

"To the yacht. It can't be too far away."

"You think you can make it?" [PAR.] "If Gertrude Ederle could
swim the English Channel, I can swim to my yacht."

"What kind of grease is that?"

"I didn't have any grease. This is honey sap from a
tree."

Bertrille touches his arm with a finger, then tastes
it. "Mmm, good. Well, I wish you luck, but I think you'll
have trouble."

"Why?"

"You're drawing flies."

And he is. A horde of flies. As Bertrille walks
back toward the other encampment, Carlos is dashing madly
here and there, finally into the ocean, trying to get rid
of the flies. FLIP.

Night has fallen. Bertrille and Estella by the fire, Bertrille trying to iron her now-repaired and starched coronet with hot rocks bound in cocoanut leaves. As they talk, Estella reveals herself to be a fortune-hunter. Without knowing that Bertrille knows Carlos, nor that Carlos is on the other side of the island, she expresses her wishes to hook "someone who can give me nothing but the best".

Bertrille queries her on love, and Estella makes it plain that she considers herself a valuable commodity (and she is a staggering looking woman) for which the buyer will have to pay dearly.

Bertrille is now confronted with the problem of keeping this piranha fish of a gold-digger away from Carlos.

FLIP to Carlos sleeping on the beach as Bertrille comes upon him. The ants are eating him, which would not have happened had he built a hammock such as Bertrille's. She suggests he use hers, as she is going to sleep on the other side of the island.

She leaves him and he gets into the hammock.

Then he starts castigating himself for being a swine. To let a young girl like that, and a Sister to boot, sleep out in the cold, while he takes her hammock. He decides to follow her. Bertrille counted on just this. We see her peering out of the foliage as he trudges in the direction she went. Bertrille takes a short cut, and gets back to Estella. She knows Carlos will stumble upon them, and she begins engaging Estella in a kind of conversation that will patently reveal the girl to be the crud she is.

Finally, Carlos steps out of the bushes, as Estella makes her plans for him known.

He is gentleman enough to refrain from calling her the names she deserves.

But Bertrille has saved him from himself.

At that moment, up comes a night breeze. Bertrille feels it first, grabs her coronet, and starts running back toward the first encampment with Carlos. They lose Estella in the underbrush. She must not know Bertrille can fly.

When they get back to the first locale, Carlos is worried about her flying at night. Bertrille assures him she will be all right, and as Estella breaks into the clearing, Bertrille is already rising.

Estella comes to Carlos, who is coldly, distantly polite to her. She asks what that strange white bird was. "A bird of paradise," Carlos says.

                                        FADE OUT.

ELLISON / 15

(NOTE: the author submits two (2) count 'em two (2) TAG
ending possibilities. The Omniscient Producer may pick the
one of his choice.)


TAG I:

Bertrille flies up, encounters a night-flying plane
(Stock) and with a bit of crayon from her habit, or berry-
juice from the island((whichever serves best will be
established at the outset of segment)) writes on the port
of the small plane:

        S.O.S.  PEOPLE ON ISLAND BELOW.  HELP!

FLIP TO pilot on radio saying to tower, "How do I
know how it got there...maybe flying saucers...maybe gremlins
...all I know is it wasn't there when I took off."

And Bertrille, smiling to herself, returning via air
route to San Tanco, while on the island Carlos tells the
girl they will be rescued soon. Estella wants to know how
he knows. "A little kind-of-bird told me," he says.

Close on Bertrille winging in to the convent and
           FADE OUT.

TAG II:

Bertrille alighting the next morning, out of sight.
She emerges from the brush and hears Carlos being very cool
and polite to Estella. We know <u>absolutely</u> <u>nothing</u> happened
between them during the night. Not with what Carlos
knows about her.

Estella is trying to get into Carlos' good graces
again. He is saying something terribly self-revealing
about himself:

"There are most times when I am a silly playboy.
I get too much involved with the good life to know it
is no life at all. I consider myself very lucky only to
have paid the price of one yacht to learn the lesson you
taught me about a certain kind of woman."

Bertrille emerges, and says hi everybody.

Carlos is relieved and pleased to see her.

Estella is sour.

"Look," says Bertrille, "here comes a boat!"

Stock shot out on the water. A boat is indeed coming.

Bertrille looks sad.

"Why so unhappy?" asks Carlos. "We're going home."

"I know. But next I was going to have you build me
a tree house, Friday. And a comb from a conch shell, and
a shower from bamboo, and..."

As she raves on, Carlos looks toward Heaven and we

                                              FADE OUT.

<u>"YOU CAN'T GET THERE FROM HERE"</u>

written by Harlan Ellison

#3530


<u>TEASER</u>

FADE IN:


<u>EXT. SISTER BERTRILLE AGAINST BLUE SKY — DAY</u>

1     Skimming along through the cloudless sky. (STOCK)

2     ANGLE PAST BERTRILLE — THE ISLAND
As she looks down, we see she is flying over the
Ocean, and the island is down there, <u>way</u> down there.
(Suggest matte shot.)

             SISTER JACQUELINE'S VOICE (o.s.)
The sirens of summer had sung sweetly to
Sister Bertrille who was, despite her,
uh, special abilities, still only a young
girl on a lovely day. She had gone aloft
for a brief flight...

3     ANOTHER ANGLE ON BERTRILLE
As she does a roll, a dip, a turn, an Immelmann.

             SISTER BERTRILLE
          (makes sounds like a
          WWI plane & machine gun)
Take <u>that</u>, Red Baron! And nuts to the
Kaiser, <u>too</u>!

             SISTER JACQUELINE'S VOICE (o.s.)
...and she had ventured perhaps <u>too</u> far
from San Juan. And when the winds fell,
very suddenly...

4     WITH BERTRILLE
As she starts to drop very suddenly, toward the
island.
             SR. BERTRILLE
          (panics)
Whooop, whooop, whooop

As she vanishes from the frame.

5     AERIAL VIEW (STOCK)
      Of Bertrille descending.  Not falling, but not able
      to stay aloft either.  A rapid, semi-controlled descent.

EXT. JUNGLE ISLAND - DAY

6     UP-ANGLE INTO LOW TREE
      surrounded by underbrush that features plants with
      cactus-like spines and a good springy mattress of
      bushes, as Bertrille comes "whoop-whoop-whooooping"
      down out of the sky, and plunges into the tree-top,
      which breaks her fall.  Her coronet, however, is
      snatched from her head, out of frame.  CAMERA TILTS
      DOWN with Bertrille as she bounces down through the
      leafy tree-top into the bushes and thence into the
      spined plants, with a crash and a howl.

7     INSERT SHOT (STOCK)
      exotic birds giving one hell of squawk as they rise
      up and shriek away.  Implication: Bertrille has
      startled them.

8     MEDIUM-CLOSE SHOT - BERTRILLE
      Lying very unladylike in the bushes, making a sour
      face and hearing the sounds of birds, not all of
      which are outside her head.  CAMERA MOVES BACK as
      she rises, feels the pain of the nettle spines,
      extricates several in a broadly humorous manner,
      and comes out of the bushes.  She looks up and
      down the beach as we

                                        INTERCUT WITH:

9     INTERCUTS - BEACH - DAY - (STOCK)
      the surf rolling in, the sand, the jungle, emptiness.

                                        CUT BACK TO:

10    ANGLE SHOT PAST BERTRILLE
      with the jungle behind her.  As she turns and turns
      and looks at her predicament.

                         SR. BERTRILLE
                           (sincerely)
                  I just hate this a lot.

      Then she sees something.  CAMERA PULLS BACK TO EXPAND
      ANGLE as she hurries to the water's edge and looks
      down.

11    INSERT SHOT
      the coronet.  Washing gently in and out with the waves.
      It is badly torn, dirty, soaked into a shapeless mass.
      She picks it up.

12  REACTION SHOT - BERTRILLE
as she realizes her flying is over for the time being.
A play of emotions crosses her extremely mobile face.
We see exasperation, concern, trepidation, and finally
just a touch of fear.  She looks all around, and then
cups her hands to her mouth and shouts.

                    SR. BERTRILLE
                      (yelling)
          Anybody here?  Hey, anybody!
                      (listens)
          Nice island you've got here!
                      (listens; no answer;
                       shrugs; to herself)
          Maybe it's livelier on Saturday
          nights.

13  FULL SHOT - STRIP OF BEACH - FAVORING BERTRILLE
As her second shrug tells us she is resigned to making
the best of it.  She wrings out the coronet, pulls a
length of vine from a tree, ties it between two bushes,
and hangs the coronet on it neatly, to dry.  CAMERA
MOVES IN as she begins a very businesslike gathering
of small twigs and bits of driftwood.  She piles them
in the sand, and then starts rubbing two sticks
together in a rapid movement.  Nothing happens.  No
spark.  She tries again, faster.  Still nothing.

                    SR. BERTRILLE
          Instant fire: merely add fire.

She throws down the sticks, gets up, brushes herself
off, and starts looking around for something that
will burn better.  Seeing nothing, she moves up the
beach a little ways.  She is looking down in the
sand.  Suddenly she stops.  Her eyes widen.

14  INSERT SHOT
a large, obviously male, footprint.  Bare foot.  She
is wearing shoes.  She puts her foot next to the print.
It is twice the size of her shoe.

15  CLOSEUP - BERTRILLE
Suddenly having thoughts of headhunters.

                    SISTER JACQUELINE'S VOICE (o.s.)
                In situations like that, there are
                only two thoughts: do the natives
                still make hero sandwiches out of
                missionaries...
                      (beat)
                ...and...are the natives restless
                tonight?

CAMERA HOLDS on Bertrille's comical look of terror.

                                        FADE OUT.

## ACT ONE

FADE IN:

## ESTABLISHING SHOT - THE ISLAND (STOCK)

16    LONG SHOT MOVING IN ON BERTRILLE - LOW ANGLE
Shooting low from sand CLOSE ON FOOTPRINT at rising
angle to Bertrille in b.g. coming steadily along the
trail of footprints TOWARD CAMERA. When she dominates
frame in med-CLOSEUP, her expression of fear and expectation
alters to one of surprise. BIG REACTION FROM BERTRILLE.

17    REVERSE ANGLE - BERTRILLE'S POV - WHAT SHE SEES
Sitting on a rock near the edge of the water, tossing
pebbles into the Ocean, is CARLOS RAMIREZ. He is
dressed in white dinner jacket, tuxedo slacks, very
dashing, but barefoot. He looks disconsolate.

18    TWO-SHOT - BERTRILLE & CARLOS
as she squeals with delight. He turns and sees her.

>          SR. BERTRILLE
>            (delighted)
>    Mr. Ramirez!

He does not reply, merely closes his eyes tightly, then
opens them as if not expecting to see her. When he
does see her, he begins nodding his head steadily, in
a resigned manner (if he was Yiddish, he would be
duhvening). She speaks to him again, as she moves
toward him.

>          SR. BERTRILLE
>            (querulous)
>    Mr. Ramirez?

She comes to him. He is staring out to sea, nodding his
head. He does not speak. She hunkers down beside him.

>          SR. BERTRILLE
>            (xtreme bright)
>    Hi!

>          CARLOS
>         (soft, sad)
>    Some men get washed up on
>    desert islands with Brigitte
>    Bardot...some men get cast
>    adrift with Vanessa Redgrave...
>    some men are castaway even with
>    perhaps Phyllis Diller and they
>    can't complain.
>        (beat)
>    Me...I get you. Always you!
>    Are you haunting me, Sister?

>                      (CONTINUED:)

18    CONTINUED:

> SR. BERTRILLE
> (after a beat)
> You're raving.

> CARLOS
> (pouts)
> I'm unhappy.

She sits down beside him, and begins lobbing pebbles
into the sea, even as he is doing it. Silence. Then
each turns to the other at the same instant, each
begins to speak, both lapse into silence awkwardly.
Silence for a beat, then Carlos tries again:

> CARLOS
> Where is your coronet? You
> can fly out for help.

> SR. BERTRILLE
> It got torn. I can't fly.

Silence again. Then Bertrille tries, smiling.

> SR. BERTRILLE
> We're not in any trouble: we
> can take your yacht. We're saved!

Carlos shakes his head.

> CARLOS
> (matter-of-fact)
> Wrong.

> SR. BERTRILLE
> Wrong?

> CARLOS
> (definite)
> Wrong.

> SR. BERTRILLE
> Why?

> CARLOS
> (sheepish)
> I've been marooned.

> SR. BERTRILLE
> (amazed, wide-eyed)
> By a mutinous crew of bloodthirsty
> cutthroats?

(CONTINUED:)

18    CONTINUED: - 2

Carlos looks toward Heaven, he is ashamed.

                    CARLOS
                (shakes head)
        By Estella Ruiz.

                    SR. BERTRILLE
        She cast you adrift?

                    CARLOS
        She threw me overboard.

                    SR. BERTRILLE
        She was bigger than you.

                    CARLOS
        She moved faster than me.

19    CLOSE ON BERTRILLE - CARLOS BEHIND HER

So we have both their faces in profile.  Carlos speaks,
but all the reactions are on Bertrille's face.

                    CARLOS
        I, uh, met her at the club, and
        suggested we could, uh, get to
        know each other better on a
        little sail out here alone.

                    SR. BERTRILLE
        Estella Ruiz.

                    CARLOS
        Estella Ruiz.

Bertrille now has an expression of scorn on her face.
She has read between Carlos' words.  She knows what
he had in mind.  Carlos hurries on, trying to explain
and vindicate himself.

                    CARLOS
        We had a picnic planned, and when
        we got here, well, I, uh, tried
        to, well you might say, _solidify_
        our friendship.
                (beat, woeful)
        She pushed me over the side and
        took the yacht.

                    SR. BERTRILLE
        Estella Ruiz.

                                        (CONTINUED:)

19    CONTINUED:

>>SR<< CARLOS
(sadly)
Estella Ruiz.

SR. BERTRILLE
(chiding)
Tsk-tsk.  Seems like you were
out-maneuvered this time.

CARLOS
It isn't charitable to gloat
over a man's misfortune.

SR. BERTRILLE
Somehow, I can't feel too sorry
for you.
(beat)
Well!  We've got to make do the
best we can.

Carlos looks at her.  What is she talking about?

20    ANOTHER ANGLE - FULL FRONT SHOT - CARLOS & BERTRILLE

as Bertrille works herself into the mood of their situation.

SR. BERTRILLE
Survival is the important thing.
Here we are, two lonely castaways
on a terror-filled island lost in
the empty ocean.
(dramatic)
It'll be tooth and nail if we expect
to live out the years till a chance
merchantman stumbles on us here.

CARLOS
(as if she's nuts)
What're you talking about?  As soon
as that Estella feels enough remorse
she'll turn around and come back.
(folds arms)
I'm going to sit here and wait for
her.

Bertrille leaps to her feet, aroused.

SR. BERTRILLE
That's the _worst_ thing you can do!

(CONTINUED:)

20    CONTINUED:

> CARLOS
> Now you're raving.

> SR. BERTRILLE
> But...but...we're like Robinson
> Crusoe and Friday! We've got
> to make preparations for a long
> stay.

> CARLOS
> The only preparations I'm making,
> Sister, are to make Estella Ruiz
> sorry she ever ran off with my
> yacht!

He clenches and unclenches his hands as though holding
Estella Ruiz's neck. But Bertrille won't quit.

> SR. BERTRILLE
> You don't know what we might face
> here! Wild beasts. Exposure.
> The rigors of the night. Starvation.
> Dying of thirst. Berri-berri.
> Rindapest. Hoof-and-mouth disease.
> An unexpected monsoon!

> CARLOS
> (calm)
> Monsoons don't occur in these
> latitudes.

> SR. BERTRILLE
> (carols)
> See? See how unexpected it would be?!

Carlos rolls his eyes.

> CARLOS
> Will you stop nagging me if I
> cooperate, Sister?

Bertrille nods happily. Carlos gets up, brushes off
his clothes, looks resigned.

> SR. BERTRILLE
> The first thing is to get a big
> signal fire going. Firewood!
> You go that way...
>         (she points up beach)
> ...and I'll go this way...
>         (points down beach)
> and gather up as much as you can.

21    MED. LONG SHOT - THE BEACH

as Bertrille strides off one way, Carlos throws arms
up in resignation, and goes off in other direction.

FLIP-FRAME TO:

22    BEACH - DAY - MEDIUM SHOT ON CARLOS

staggering up beach toward us, awkwardly clutching
a load of sticks and tree refuse. He is dropping more
than he's carrying, which isn't a great deal. He
keeps stooping down awkwardly to retrieve the latest
droppings. As he COMES TO CAMERA a look of shock
registers on his handsome face as we

PAN RAPIDLY AROUND TO:

23    BEACH - DAY - REVERSE ANGLE - WHAT HE SEES

Bertrille coming up the beach the same as he had been.
Except she is dragging a very workable little sledge
made of sticks bound together by vines. She is pulling
it by a vine rope, like a child's snow sled. It is
loaded to the top with a small mountain of fire fodder.
Carlos moves into the shot and mumbles under his breath as we

FLIP-FRAME TO:

24    XTREME CLOSEUP ON FIREWOOD PILED HIGH

pyre, as yet unlit,
as CAMERA PULLS BACK we see it is the signal fire they
had planned. Bertrille seems happy, Carlos is moody.

                    SR. BERTRILLE
            X You were a big help, Mr.
            Ramirez.

25    CLOSE ON CARLOS

a look that could kill.

26    SAME AS 24

Bertrille looks around as though seeking something.

                    SR. BERTRILLE
            Now we have to light it.

Almost absently, Carlos reaches into his jacket and
hands her his lighter. CAMERA IN to show us it is a
beautiful gold lighter inlaid with diamonds.

                    SR. BERTRILLE
            Oh, that's just great.

                              (CONTINUED:)

26    CONTINUED:

She tries to make it light several times, but it won't
catch.  She starts pulling it apart.

                    SR. BERTRILLE
               Must've gotten wet.  I'll dry
               the flint and steel.

In a second she has it apart, as Carlos stares unbelieving.
She drops the gold case in the sand.  Carlos rushes and
picks it up.

                    CARLOS
                    (affronted)
               That was given to me by a Marquessa.
               It's worth a fortune!

Bertrille's answer is in a pseudo-Humphrey Bogart
cynical tone; very hard; something out of Raymond
Chandler, perhaps.

                    SR. BERTRILLE
               Of what use is gold to us here?
               Of what use are diamonds?  Survival
               is what counts now!  Tooth and
               nail against the—

                    CARLOS
                    (yells, cuts her off)
               I know!  I know!

                    BERTRILLE
               ~~Shrugs~~ (shrugs)
               Just trying to impress you with
               the seriousness of the situation.

                    CARLOS
                    (dryly)
               Sister, you'll <u>never</u> know how you've
               impressed me.

Bertrille gathers some tinder, and tries to get it lit
with the flint and steel.  She keeps at it for a few
moments.  It won't take.

                    SR. BERTRILLE
               It won't catch.  We need something
               else.  Empty your pockets.

                    CARLOS
               What!?!  Why?

                              FLIP-FRAME TO:

27     ANOTHER ANGLE

CLOSE ON BERTRILLE'S HANDS as she peels bills off a
large roll of money.  The ones on the outside are wet.
But as she gets into the center, the bills are dry.
CAMERA PULLS BACK to show Carlos tromping up and down
behind her, as she throws wet bills off the roll in
a casual manner.  He gathers them up.

                    SR. BERTRILLE
          Hey, here's some that are still
          dry.  Aren't we lucky?

                    CARLOS
          You can't burn <u>money</u>, it's...it's...
          indecent!

Bertrille has already crumbled up a large number of
bills near the tinder, and is working with the flint
and steel.

                    SR. BERTRILLE
          Tooth and nail...

                    CARLOS
                (a little insane)
          Tooth and nail, tooth and nail...

The fire catches, the money starts to burn, Bertrille
quickly shoves it into the pile of tinder, the signal
pyre catches and CAMERA PANS ACROSS to Carlos' face.

                    CARLOS
                (softly)
          Serves me right for carrying the
          hundreds in the middle of the roll.

                              FLIP-FRAME TO:

28     EDGE OF BEACH - LATER DAY

As Bertrille comes up behind Carlos.  The signal fire
is going in the b.g.  Carlos sits on the edge of the
beach, looking extremely sad.

                    SR. BERTRILLE
          Don't be so glum, Mr. Ramirez,
          it was only about four hundred
          dollars.

                    CARLOS
          You're making an old man of me.

                              (CONTINUED:)

28   CONTINUED:

                    SR. BERTRILLE
          You're just hungry.  What you
          need is something to eat, it'll
          bounce your spirits right up!

                    CARLOS
          Sister, just let me sit here and
          think ugly thoughts about Estella
          Ruiz...please.

Bertrille bits her lip.  She is really worried about
Carlos.  Then she fumbles around in her habit, pulls
out a safety pin, and sits down beside him, bending
it.  He watches, not very interested.  Then she jumps
up again, rushes over to the firewood sledge she
built, grabs up a branch, and pulls the vine loose
that she used to pull the contrivance.  She rushes back
to Carlos, tying the vine to the end of the pole, and
attaching the safety pin to the vine.  He has been
watching with a little more interest.  She holds out
her construction proudly.

                    SR. BERTRILLE
          See?  We eat.
                    (beat)
          All you have to do is go dig me
          some worms.

Carlos leaps up.

                    CARLOS
          Worms!?!  Dig worms!?!

                    SR. BERTRILLE
                    (sarcastic)
          Whaddaya think fish eat, barbecue
          beef sandwiches?

                    CARLOS
                    (folds arms)
          I will not dig worms.

                    SR. BERTRILLE
          If we're gonna catch fish to eat,
          you've gotta dig worms.

                    CARLOS
                    (firmly)
          I will not dig worms.  It is demeaning.
          It is beneath the station of a
          gentleman of Puerto Rico to dig worms.
                    (beat)
          And besides, it'll ruin a perfectly
                    (MORE)
                                        (CONTINUED:)

28    CONTINUED: - 2

CARLOS (CONT'D)
good seven-dollar manicure.

He extends his well-tailored fingertips.  Bertrille
explodes.

SR. BERTRILLE
Listen, mister!  In this operation
nobody eats who doesn't work.  If
you think I'm going to work my
fingers to the bone while you lie
around getting a suntan, you're
sadly mistaken...
        (by this time she's
        raving)
...it's 50-50 if we're going to
defeat the elements...tooth and
nail against the...

CARLOS
(hands over ears)
All right!  All right!  I'll dig
worms!  I'll dig snakes, cobras, pythons!

He stalks off into the jungle, still mumbling the names
of reptiles he'll dig up.  Bertrille watches him go,
her hands on her hips.  Then she turns, with a flounce,
as if to say: well, he's shaping up.  She walks toward
the little tide pool near the edge of the beach.

29    MEDIUM SHOT - TIDE POOL - BERTRILLE IN B.G.

as she comes to the little pool, stands on an overhanging
rock, and drops the fishline in.  She is not there five
seconds when there is a jerk on the line, she yanks it
back up, and there's a large fish flopping and jiggling
on the end.  Bertrille grins hugely and yells:

SR. BERTRILLE
Hey!  Forget those worms!

FLIP-FRAME TO:

30    INT. JUNGLE - ON BERTRILLE

as she pushes and shoves her way through the undergrowth.

SR. BERTRILLE
(yelling)
Mr. Ramirez!  I don't need the
worms now!  Yoo-hoo, Mr. Ramirez.

CAMERA GOES WITH HER a little ways.  Nothing.

DISSOLVE THRU:

31      SERIES OF TRUCKING SHOTS - THRU JUNGLE
thru
33      WITH BERTRILLE as she calls for Carlos, plunging here
        and there, from DIFFERENT ANGLES, giving the impression
        of extensive jungle area.

                        SR. BERTRILLE
                Mr. Ramirez!  Mr. Ramirez!  Hey,
                where are you?  Ally-ally-in-free!

                                        DISSOLVE THRU TO:

34      SMALL CLEARED SPACE - DAY

        Bertrille stands at the edge of a small clearing, or
        similar area where jungle is thinned out.  She is
        looking all around her.  Nothing.

                        SR. BERTRILLE
                        (yells)
                Mr. Ramirez!  Where are you?

        A **very soft** VOICE answers her.  It cannot be stressed
        too much how **gently** this voice speaks.

                        CARLOS' VOICE (o.s.)
                Over here, Sister.

        She looks all around as CAMERA PANS WITH HER POV.  We
        see nothing.  Carlos is not in sight.

                        SR. BERTRILLE
                        (perplexed)
                **Where** are you?

                        CARLOS' VOICE (o.s.)
                        (ever so soft)
                Here.

                        SR. BERTRILLE
                        (at a loss)
                Where?

                        CARLOS' VOICE (o.s.)
                        (softer yet)
                Down here.

        Bertrille half-turns to follow sound of VOICE, and
        she looks down.  A few feet away is underbrush.  She
        reaches over, parts it, and yelps.  There is Carlos,
        up to his armpits in quicksand.  The more he talks,
        the deeper he sinks.  Bertrille starts running around
        like a nut, shrieking, paniced, reaching for him,
        almost going in herself, dashing madly here&there.

                                        (CONTINUED:)

34    CONTINUED:

Bertrille is whooping and wailing, shrieking and making
typical Bertrille-noises.  It is a Chinese fire-and-boat
drill.  Finally, exhausted from her own hysteria, she
slows down, stops, arms dangling, and panting, looks at
Carlos.

                    SR. BERTRILLE
                      (awkwardly)
          Do you, uh, have any favorite prayers?

                    CARLOS
                      (exasperated, but
                      very very softly)
          Sister, prayer isn't necessary
          right now.

He sinks a little as he speaks.  His eyes roll.

                    CARLOS (Cont'd)
                      (whispers)
          Just tie a vine around a tree and
          throw me the end...

Bertrille's face lights up, she dashes here and there,
pauses a moment to speak to him...

                    SR. BERTRILLE
          Quick thinking, partner!  Tooth
          and nail...

                    CARLOS
                      (yells)
          Yaaaaaaaaggggghhhh!

                    SR. BERTRILLE
          Right.

She dashes off as Carlos sinks a little more.

                                        FLIP-FRAME TO:

35    SAME AS 27 - NEAR SIGNAL FIRE

They sit eatingxxkim beside the signal fire, Carlos'
clothes drying on his back.  Other pieces of his dinner
outfit hang on the clothesline with her coronet.  They
each have a piece of fried fish on a large leaf before
them.  Their heads are bowed.

                    SR. BERTRILLE
          ...and thank you Lord, for the
          bounty of the sea, and for making
          us comfortable under such
          harrowing conditions.  Amen.

                                        (CONTINUED:)

35    CONTINUED:

Bertrille digs into her fish, eating voraciously, but
daintily. Carlos looks moody.

                SR. BERTRILLE
        Better eat. You'll need your
        strength.

                CARLOS
                (bitter)
        I know: tooth and nail...

                SR. BERTRILLE
                (firmly)
        You're really the grouchiest
        companion I've ever been on
        a desert island with.

                CARLOS
        I am a paragon of joy compared
        to what I'd be if that Estella
        Ruiz was here!

                SR. BERTRILLE
                (worried)
        You aren't really angry with
        her, are you?

                CARLOS
                (quietly)
        I am livid with rage.

                SR. BERTRILLE
        It's your own fault.

                CARLOS
        Nonetheless, I will wring her
        lovely neck. Slowly. With
        great care. And great joy.

                SR. BERTRILLE
        You have no one to blame but yourself.
        Luring girls onto your yacht! Sailing
        out where they can't even walk home.
        Serves you right.

                CARLOS
        Sister, I am a desolate and
        uncomfortable figure of a man
        at this moment. Kindly do not
        bug me.

                            (CONTINUED:)

35   CONTINUED: - 2

Bertrille turns into a more comfortable position.
Carlos, sensing a lecture coming, looks exasperated.

> SR. BERTRILLE
> You know, Mr. Ramirez, I've been
> looking forward to a chance for
> a long talk, with you.  Seems
> like the time is right, now.

> CARLOS
> I'm beginning to understand why
> some men become hermits.

> SR. BERTRILLE
> No, honestly, I think you have a
> real problem.

> CARLOS
>         (looks at her
>          pointedly)
> I would call that a perceptive
> analysis of the situation.

> SR. BERTRILLE
> I don't think you understand women
> at all.

Carlos turns on her.  He holds up his hand for her to stop.

> CARLOS
> Sister, you can make me dig worms,
> burn my money, bury me in quicksand,
> but kindly, <u>kindly</u> do not shatter
> my self-image.  Allow me to continue
> living in a fool's paradise!

> SR. BERTRILLE
> I'm only trying to help.

> CARLOS
> You have helped me more today than
> I have any right to expect.  It may
> take me <u>years</u> to repay you.

Bertrille shrugs.  Okay, if that's the way you want it,
Carlos.  She polishes off the fish, washes her hands
in the water, buries the fish bones and gets up.

> SR. BERTRILLE
> We'd better make arrangements
> for sleeping tonight.

36    ANOTHER ANGLE — FULL SHOT

as Carlos rises, hurling what's left of his fish out
into the water.  He brushes himself off.

> CARLOS
> Do as you like.  I don't
> intend to sleep here tonight.

> SR. BERTRILLE
> You may have to.

> CARLOS
> (firm)
> Sister, I do not wish to discuss
> it further.

He turns away.

> SR. BERTRILLE
> (quashed)
> Okay, if you don't want to help.
> If you don't work, you don't
> get any of the benefits.

Carlos does not answer.  Bertrille shrugs, walks to the
edge of the jungle and begins pulling down vines as we

DISSOLVE TO:

37    ANGLE ON JUNGLE-EDGE — LATER DAY

as Bertrille completes the last weave of the hammock.
It is crude, but effective.  It hangs between two
small trees and looks extremely comfortable.  She
tests it with her hands, and when she thinks it is
firm, she very cautiously sits in it.  It supports her
weight.  She swings up her legs.  She bounces.  Then
she gets out of it, and goes to Carlos.

> SR. BERTRILLE
> Well, now that that's taken care
> of, Friday—

> CARLOS
> (snaps)
> Don't call me Friday!

> SR. BERTRILLE
> Sorry.  Just fooling.
> (beat)
> Uh, Mr. Ramirez: we'll need fresh
> drinking water.

(CONTINUED:)

37    CONTINUED:

Carlos looks up at the sun, and licks his lips. With
great reluctance he nods his head. He hates to admit
she may be right.

                    CARLOS
          I suppose so.

                    SR. BERTRILLE
          Right. Now you go up the beach,
          I'll go down the beach, around
          the island. Look for where the
          foliage is the greenest, that's
          where there ought to be fresh
          water.

He nods agreement, and they each start off in the
direction indicated, with Carlos yelling back over
his shoulder:
                    CARLOS
          But the yacht will be here any
          time now! I'm only going
          because I'm thirsty!

CAMERA PULLS UP AND AWAY as they walk away from each
other on the beach. CAMERA PICKS UP the hot glow of
the sun and as it fills the frame we
                              LAP-DISSOLVE TO:

38    ANOTHER ANGLE ON BEACH

FRAME FILLED WITH SUNGLOW that MATCHES PRECEDING SHOT.
As CAMERA ANGLE DESCENDS we see Bertrille walking
alone through the jungle. Transition from sc. 37 to
sc. 38 tells us she has been moving around the island.
CAMERA COMES DOWN to MEDIUM-LONG SHOT OF HER.

39    CLOSE SHOT — ON BERTRILLE

CAMERA ZOOMS IN on her FACE just as she turns to look
into CAMERA. Stark terror fills her face. She yelps.

40    REVERSE ANGLE — BERTRILLE'S POV — WHAT SHE SEES

CAMERA ZOOM DUPLICATES EFFECT OF SC. 39. IN FAST on
a small tide pool with rocks around the edge (redress
tide pool sc. 29). Something is crawling out of
the water. It looks like the Creature From The Black
Lagoon to us. It is covered with seaweed and moss.
It rises up and up.

41    TWO-SHOT — BERTRILLE & "CREATURE"

as she backs up, hands over mouth, petrified with
fear, she takes two steps, falls over a rock, and
lands in awkward sitting position, unable to move
as Creature comes toward her, lumberingly.

42    UP-ANGLE SHOT - PAST BERTRILLE TO "CREATURE"

Bertrille large in f.g. as Creature menacingly advances
on her, till it towers over her. Bertrille is making
tiny little queeping noises. Then, when the thing is
almost upon her, it reaches up, parts the seaweed, and
we suddenly see it is a beautiful blonde girl in a
bikini. It is, of course, ESTELLA RUIZ.

>                    ESTELLA
>          Who're you?

>                    SR. BERTRILLE
>               (relieved, but stunned)
>          I...I...I'm Sister Bertrille, from
>          the Convent of San Tanco...what're
>          ...uh...who're you?

>                    ESTELLA
>          I'm Estella. Wheew, what a swim!

She starts pulling off the seaweed. Bertrille regains
her feet and CAMERA ELEVATES ACCORDINGLY to FULL 2-SHOT.

>                    SR. BERTRILLE
>          Queeps, I thought sure you were
>          going to make a Bertrille-burger
>          out of me...
>               (her mouth drops open)
>          Estella?

Estella nods.

>                    SR. BERTRILLE
>          From the yacht Estella?

Estella nods again.

>                    SR. BERTRILLE
>               (capering)
>          Hurray! We're saved! Where is
>          it? How soon can we leave?

>                    ESTELLA
>          As soon as we can get to your boat.

>                    SR. BERTRILLE
>          My boat? I thought we'd use your
>          boat?

>                    ESTELLA
>          That would be difficult.

(CONTINUED:)

42     CONTINUED:

CAMERA FAVORS BERTRILLE. She claps her hands over her
ears, squinches up her face.

> SR. BERTRILLE
> Don't say it!

> ESTELL'
> I sank it.

Bertrille drops hands, looks at her, sick.

> SR. BERTRILLE
> (pathetic)
> I asked you not to say it.

CAMERA HOLDS ON HER PAINED EXPRESSION as we

>                    FADE OUT.


<u>END ACT ONE</u>

ACT TWO

FADE IN:

EXT. (STOCK) - THE ISLAND - DAY

43    ESTABLISHING SHOT.

44    BOOM SHOT - EXT. JUNGLE - DESCENDING - BERTRILLE & ESTELLA

They are busily engaged in erecting a simple, but
effective lean-to. CAMERA COMES DOWN TO THEM thru
the leaves of the trees, till we HOLD THEM in MEDIUM
LONG SHOT.

> SR. JACQUELINE'S VOICE (o.s.)
> Sister Crusoe, er, Sister Bertrille now
> had a double problem. Not only could
> she not fly out for help, but she had
> decided Carlos Ramirez's attitude
> toward the girl who had taken his
> yacht was, well, less than friendly.
> (beat)
> She now had two communities of
> survival going, one on either side
> of the island, and neither knew about
> the other. But...night was coming.

CAMERA TO THEM at this point.

> ESTELLA
> I still don't see why we can't
> use the camp with the fire. I
> can see it from here.

> SR. BERTRILLE
> (hastily)
> Uh...we can't use it because of
> the, uh, because of the...the
> vampire bugs!

> ESTELLA
> (horrified)
> Vampire bugs!?!

> SR. BERTRILLE
> (improvising rapidly)
> Uh, right, right. Oh, they're
> awful. Big as sparrows. They
> get drawn by the fire. They, uh,
> really bite...bleed you white!

(CONTINUED:)

44    CONTINUED:

Estella shivers with dusgust.

                    ESTELLA
          Yeccchhh!

                    SR. BERTRILLE
          Don't worry about it.  I'll go
          over there every once in a while
          and keep the fire up.

                    ESTELLA
          But what about the vampire bugs?
          Won't they bite you?

Bertrille holds up her rosary, with an impish grin.

                    SR. BERTRILLE
          They wouldn't dare.

                                        FLIP-FRAME TO:

45    ANGLE THRU JUNGLE WITH BERTRILLE

CLOSE BEHIND HER as she comes out of the jungle, pushing
aside the foliage.  In a LONG SHOT we see Carlos,
running to the water's edge, dashing back onto the sand,
running in circles, then back to the water, onto the
sand, running in circles, etcetera, over and over.
He's barefoot, and really dashing around like a nut.
Bertrille walks down toward him as CAMERA STAYS WITH HER.

46    ANOTHER ANGLE

as Bertrille stands to one side, watching him in his
wild maneuvers.  Her arms are folded.  She watches
with mild interest.  Finally, exhausted, panting,
Carlos stops in front of her.

                    SR. BERTRILLE
          Get a nice workout?

                    CARLOS
                  (panting)
          I'm saving our lives!

                    SR. BERTRILLE
          All right, I'll play your little
          game: how are you saving our lives?

                    CARLOS
                  (points)
          By getting my feet wet and dragging
          them in the sand, I've made a huge
          S.O.S.              (CONTINUED:)

46    CONTINUED:

Bertrille looks past him, nods appreciation of his
work, but there is something impish in her look.

> SR. BERTRILLE
> Ran back and forth a lot, huh?

> CARLOS
> (proudly)
> For a man of indomitable will,
> there is always a way out!

> SR. BERTRILLE
> Wet feet...big S.O.S., right?

> CARLOS
> (puffs up)
> Skill and cunning instinct will
> always win the day.

> SR. BERTRILLE
> Haven't had much experience at
> this cunning instinct, have you?

> CARLOS
> (reluctantly)
> No, not much, but so what?

Bertrille points.

> SR. BERTRILLE
> You misspelled it.

47    LONG SHOT FROM ABOVE - S.O.S. IN SAND

as Carlos stands staring at it, Bertrille walks away,
back into the jungle. This is a high shot that looks
down on the message walked-into the wet sand. It is
spelled:

> S. S. O.

> FLIP-FRAME TO:

48    ESTELLA'S CAMPSITE - DAY

CLOSE ON HANDS STRIPPING VINE into thin threads.
CAMERA BACK to show us it is Estella, stripping the
tough vines into little threads. Bertrille is
sitting cross-legged, using a needle made from a
sliver of wood and a vine-thread, sewing up her
coronet. The coronet is still a limp rag, though
dry. It is already cross-hatched with repairs.

> (CONTINUED:)

48      CONTINUED:

                          ESTELLA
              Sister Bertrille, I still
              cannot understand why we
              spend so much time repairing
              your coronet.

                          SR. BERTRILLE
              Well, I, uh, just don't feel
              quite right with my habit
              incomplete. Darn it!

The vine has broken.  Estella holds up her hands.

                          ESTELLA
              The vines are tough, my hands
              are getting cut up.  And if
              ---as you say---we are going to
              starch the coronet, the vines
              won't hold.  We'll need something
              more like thread.

Bertrille purses her lips.  Resigned, she reaches down
and rips off a big piece of her garment.

                          SR. BERTRILLE
              How about this?

                                          FLIP-FRAME TO:

49      CARLOS' CAMPSITE - WITH BERTRILLE

as she comes down the beach toward him.  He is stripped
down to his bathing trunks, rubbing some kind of sticky
substance on his chest and arms from a big leaf filled
with the glop.  Bertrille comes up to him.

                          SR. BERTRILLE
              What're you doing now?

                          CARLOS
                  (still rubbing)
              I'm greasing myself down for a
              long swim.

                          SR. BERTRILLE
              Where to?

                          CARLOS
              To the yacht.  It can't be too
              far away.  Anything is better
              than waiting.

                                          (CONTINUED:)

49    CONTINUED:

He continues rubbing the glutinous slop on his body.
Bertrille shades her eyes from the sun.

> SR. BERTRILLE
> Still ticked-off at that girl,
> huh?

> CARLOS
> (venomously)
> I would rub her down with this
> sap and stake her out for the
> ants! If I got my hands on her!

> SR. BERTRILLE
> That's what I thought—you're
> still ticked-off.

He applies a thick coat to his right arm.  Bertrille
watches, fascinated.

> SR. BERTRILLE
> Think you can make it?

> CARLOS
> If Gertrude Ederle can swim the
> English Channel, I can swim to
> my yacht.

> SR. BERTRILLE
> What kind of grease is that?

> CARLOS
> I didn't have any grease.  This
> is honey sap from a tree.

Bertrille touches his arm with a finger, then tastes it.

> SR. BERTRILLE
> Mmm, good.  Well, I wish you luck,
> but personally I think you'll have
> trouble.

> CARLOS
> Why?

> SR. BERTRILLE
> You're drawing flies.

CAMERA PULLS BACK AND UP as in sc. 47 as Carlos looks
around and the SOUND OF FLIES RISES OVER.  He begins
swatting at himself, as Bertrille walks away again.
As she leaves scene he is running amuck, swatting and
slapping at himself; finally he dashes into ocean as we

FLIP-FRAME TO:

50    ESTELLA'S CAMPSITE - NIGHT

CLOSE ON HANDS dipping the coronet---now thoroughly
mended---in a half cocoanut shell filled with cocoanut
milk.  CAMERA PULLS BACK to show Estella and Bertrille
near a small campfire, and several cocoanuts opened
around them.

                    SR. BERTRILLE
          All I have to do is soak my
          coronet in cocoanut milk and
          let it dry, and it's all
          starched.  The milk is about
          ninety per cent starch.

                    ESTELLA
               (wondering)
          How do you know these things?

                    SR. BERTRILLE
          You'd be surprised how much you
          know, without knowing you know
          it, until you need it.  I just
          remembered, that's all...tubers,
          roots, the Sago Palm...all of
          them are starch-high.

                    ESTELLA
               (wistful)
          I wish I knew things that were
          useful like that.

                    SR. BERTRILLE
          I'm sure you know a <u>lot</u> of things
          that are useful.

                    ESTELLA
               (cynically)
          I know how to make myself up so a
          man will find me attractive.  I
          know how to lure a man with smiles
          and frowns so he'll buy me things.
               (beat)
          No, Sister, I'm afraid each of us
          has learned from different teachers.

Bertrille listens to this with sudden interest.  She
continues working at dipping the coronet, but her
conversation draws Estella out more and more.

                    SR. BERTRILLE
          You never really told me how
          you came to be washed up here.

51    ANGLE ON ESTELLA

Showing her face, quite beautiful, but rather hard,
in the flickering glow of the campfire.

                    ESTELLA
          A sucker, Sister. A playboy
          from San Juan. He thinks he's
          a dazzler. I was playing him
          real good, had him hooked, and
          then--

                    SR. BERTRILLE
          Yes? Then?

                    ESTELLA
              (settles into story)
          Well, I can see he's not an
          easy mark. He's been around
          a while. So I play hard to
          get. I lead him on, then I
          cool him, lead him on, cool
          him. Like that.

                    SR. BERTRILLE
          He never suspected.

                    ESTELLA
          Very pretty boys never suspect.
          They all think they're King Kong.
              (beat)
          So I let him con me into coming
          out here, and then I gave him a
          nudge overboard. I was coming
          back for him when I sank the
          yacht. Overplayed my hand.

                    SR. BERTRILLE
          What happened to him?

                    ESTELLA
          Carlos? Oh, swam to one of the
          islands I guess. He won't be
          hurting. It's me that's out a
          meal ticket.

Estella picks idly at some twigs, tosses them into the
fire, her thoughts elsewhere. Bertrille finishes
soaking the coronet, and hangs it to dry. She stands
up, brushes herself off.

                    SR. BERTRILLE
          I'm going to put some logs on the
          signal fire. Would you heat me
          half a dozen flat stones in the
          fire here, so I can iron my coronet?

                              (CONTINUED: )

51   CONTINUED:

                    ESTELLA
          Sure, Sister.

Bertrille walks away into the jungle as darkness comes
down and we

                              FLIP-FRAME TO:

52   EXT. CARLOS' CAMPSITE - NIGHT

CLOSEUP CARLOS' FACE with an ant crawling over his
nose. CAMERA PULLS BACK to show Carlos curled up on
the beach, wrapped in his dinner jacket, the ants
eating him alive. He swats at himself periodically.
Bertrille comes into the glow of the signal fire.

                    SR. BERTRILLE
          Mr. Ramirez?

He sits up, with a groan.

                    SR. BERTRILLE
          I've found myself a nice dry
          tree over on the other side.
          I just came to tell you I'm
          not going to be using the
          hammock, so it's yours if
          you want it.

                    CARLOS
          Thank you, Sister, but I don't
          think--

                    SR. BERTRILLE
                (helps him up)
          Oh, but I insist!

She walks him to the hammock. He looks at her very
suspiciously.

                    CARLOS
          Well, the ants were eating me.

                    SR. BERTRILLE
          So you see! You just snuggle
          down in there, and I'll go and
          sleep up there in that nice
          tree.

She helps him into hammock. He looks up unsurely.

                              (CONTINUED:)

52    CONTINUED:

                    CARLOS
          You're sure...

                    SR. BERTRILLE
          Sure I'm sure.
              (she starts away)
          The worst I have to worry
          about is a torrential downpour
          or maybe a prowling wild beast.
          But I'll be safe up there.
              (boat)
          Bye.  Sleep tight.

And she's gone.  CAMERA IN CLOSE ON CARLOS.  He closes eyes.

                    CARLOS
              (to himself)
          I'll sleep.

He lies there a moment.

                    CARLOS
          I will.  I'll sleep.

He twitches slightly.  His eyes open.

                    CARLOS
              (to Heaven)
          She did it to me again.

He leaps out of the hammock, looks in direction Bertrille
just went, starts after her, murmuring loudly.

                    CARLOS
          Monsoons, wild beasts.  I can't
          handle this kind of grief.

                                        CUT TO:

53    TRUCKING SHOT - WITH BERTRILLE

as she scampers through the jungle, taking a short cut.
She keeps looking behind her, stops, hears him coming.
She holds still as he passes by on the trail, and then
scampers off again through the jungle.

                              FLIP-FRAME TO:

54    ESTELLA'S CAMPSITE

as Bertrille crashes out of the jungle, looking behind
her.  She dashes up to the fire, plops down, and starts
wrapping a hot stone in palm leaves.  The coronet is
                    (MORE)
                              (CONTINUED:)

54   CONTINUED:

                    (CONT'D)
now dry, and Estella has laid it out on a flat piece of
driftwood.  Bertrille starts ironing it.

                    ESTELLA
          Why were you running, was there
          something after you?

                    SR. BERTRILLE
          Uh, er, no.  Nothing was after
          me.  I need the exercise.  Build
          up the calf muscles...
                    (beat)
          So, uh, go on with your story.

                    ESTELLA
                    (confused)
          What story?

                    SR. BERTRILLE
          The one you were telling me.
          About that silly playboy from
          San Juan.

                    ESTELLA
          I never said he was from San Juan.

                    SR. BERTRILLE
          Oh, you didn't?  Uh, well, you
          said Puerto Rico, and I suppose
          I just assumed.  I mean, a playboy
          would have to be from San Juan,
          wouldn't he?

                    ESTELLA
                    (laughs)
          You're a funny person to be a
          Sister.

                    SR. BERTRILLE
          Yes, well...uh, I've often wondered
          if maybe a life of glamour like
          yours wasn't a better idea...

                    ESTELLA
                    (dead serious)
          Don't you believe it, Sister.
          I've been on my own since I was
          fifteen.  Making a living from
          men is no way to survive.

                              (CONTINUED:)

54    CONTINUED: - 2

Bertrille tosses out the first stone, grabs up a second
hot one, wraps it in leaves as she did the first,
and continues ironing the coronet.  She looks nervous,
glances into the jungle; we hear no sound from there.

                    ESTELLA
          Take this clown Ramirez, from
          San Juan.  He thinks all women
          are stupid, that he knows
          everything about them, which way
          they'll jump; that's why he
          gets taken by them so often.

                    SR. BERTRILLE
                 (suddenly worried)
          But, uh, he was a nice guy,
          wasn't he?

                    ESTELLA
                 (shrugs)
          How can a man trying to use
          women be a nice guy.  He was
          just another poor fish.  It's
          a shame he got away.

There is a SOUND from behind them.  CAMERA WHIP-PANS
ACROSS to show Carlos standing there.  His face is
in shadow, but as he moves out where we can see him,
his expression is not one of anger, or hatred.  It
is at once cold with restrained emotion, and filled
with the kind of pain that only comes with self-
discovery.  He moves fully into the light.  Estella
gasps and leaps up.  Bertrille comes between them.

                    CARLOS
                 (very soft)
          Thank you, Sister.  It was a
          lesson I desperately needed
          to learn.

Estella looks back and forth between them, first first
at Carlos, then at the little nun, then back to Carlos.

                    SR. BERTRILLE
                 (to Estella)
          I'm sorry...he's my friend...
          he needed to know...

Suddenly, she stops speaking, lifts her head, her eyes
widen.  She licks a finger, extends it into the air.

55      SERIES OF XTREME CLOSEUPS - THE THREE PEOPLE
thru
57      BERTRILLE as he eyes widen and she realizes:

                    SR. BERTRILLE
              The wind...it's rising!

                    CARLOS
              A night breeze...

                    ESTELLA
              What?  What is it?

58      FULL SHOT - FAVORING BERTRILLE

        as she grabs up her now fully-ironed, crosshatched but
        repaired coronet.  She grabs Carlos by the other hand,
        and begins to drag him away down the beach.  He resists
        at first, still looking at Estella, but as Bertrille
        becomes more insistent, he allows himself to be tugged,
        and then he is following quickly, their hands linked.

59      TRUCKING SHOT - WITH THEM

        as they run pell-mell up the beach toward the signal
        fire campsite.

60      CARLOS' CAMPSITE

        as they plunge to a stop, panting.  Bertrille starts
        to adjust her coronet on her head.  Carlos is gauging
        the wind.

                    CARLOS
              It's rising.

                    SR. BERTRILLE
              Can you tell which way the updraft
              will take me?

                    CARLOS
                 (feels wind with
                  outstretched hand)
              Toward San Juan, I think.  I'm
              not sure, but I think so.

                    SR. BERTRILLE
              Okay, I'm ready.

        He turns to her.  For a second they are both silent.
        Sr. Bertrille looks sad.  She wishes now that Carlos
        had never needed to know.  He looks back at her with
        tenderness.

                              (CONTINUED:)

60    CONTINUED:

                              CARLOS
                    Be careful...

                              SR. BERTRILLE
                    Carlos, I'm--I'm terribly sorry...

                              CARLOS
                    Flying at night is dangerous.

                              SR. BERTRILLE
                         (pulls self together)
                    I'll be okay.  It's a strong wind.

                              CARLOS
                         (nods)
                    And we'll be okay here, I promise.
                    ⅀ Just fly safely home.

                              SR. BERTRILLE
                    I'll send help as soon as I--

But she is already starting to rise.  He moves back as
she begins to ascend.

61    SHOT THRU JUNGLE - WITH ESTELLA

as she comes bursting through to the beach.  In the
darkness we can see something large and white rising,
but we cannot tell what it is.  She sees Carlos and
comes running down the beach toward him.  He is
standing there, unmoving, staring at the sky. She
stares up also.

                              ESTELLA
                    Carlos...I didn't know...

                              CARLOS
                         (looking up)
                    Flying at night can be dangerous.

She gives him a peculiar look, then she stares into the
sky again.

                              ESTELLA
                    What kind of bird was that?
                    So big, very strange.

                              CARLOS
                    A bird of paradise.

62    EXT. AERIAL SHOT (STOCK) - BERTRILLE - NIGHT

as she flies away toward San Tanco, we

                                        FADE OUT.


                         END ACT TWO

<u>TAG</u>

FADE IN:

<u>EXT. AERIAL SHOT (STOCK) -- NIGHT</u>

63    ANGLE ON NIGHT-FLYING PLANE

as it wheels through the darkness.

64    ANGLE CLOSE ON BERTRILLE -- NIGHT

as she rises, the wind blowing at her.

65    INT. CABIN OF PLANE -- NIGHT

PILOT alone at controls. It is a small plane, with a
window at his right. He is staring straight ahead.
Suddenly the face of Bertrille appears in the window.
The wind is blowing at her. He doesn't see her there.
She takes out a crayon from her habit, and begins
writing backwards on the window. From where we sit
it says:      S.O.S.  ISLAND BELOW  HELP!

Then she TAPS ON WINDOW LOUD. As he turns, she
vanishes. CAMERA CLOSE ON MESSAGE and his incredulous
expression.

                                        CUT TO:

66    ANOTHER AERIAL VIEW OF BERTRILLE -- (STOCK)

as she drops and skims away in the darkness.

                                        CUT TO:

67    SAME AS 65

Pilot at radio. He is speaking frantically, though
we can't hear him at first, because of wind.  Then:

                    PILOT
          How do I know how it got there...
          I tell ye it wasn't there when I
          took off...maybe flying saucers...
          maybe gremlins...the same to you,
          wise guy!

                                        CUT TO:

68     CARLOS' CAMPSITE - NIGHT

Estella and Carlos are still standing staring up.

> CARLOS
> We will be rescued, very soon.

> ESTELLA
> How do <u>you</u> know?

> CARLOS
> (very sober)
> A little kind-of-bird told me.

CUT TO:

69     AERIAL VIEW OF BERTRILLE - NIGHT - (STOCK)

the little nun, winging her way back home against
the light of the stars as we

FADE TO BLACK

and

FADE OUT.

THE END

Two from Nowhere

## Editor's Note: The Man Who Contorted Himself
## Around Copyright Laws to Earth

In 1977, *The Man Who Fell to Earth* fell in Harlan Ellison's lap. Well, not *The Man Who Fell to Earth*, per se, but something almost but not quite exactly like that 1976 cinematic adaptation of Walter Tevis's 1963 novel. (From the month Tevis's first story "The Hustler" appeared in *Playboy*—later, the novel, then the famous movie—Harlan and his friend Walter...shot pool many times.) Ellison being Ellison, demured, assuring the suits that he would—with certainty—savage the material on hand as derivative twaddle, but they insisted he "take" a meeting to "open up everyone's thinking."

Having duly savaged the derivative twaddle, Ellison determined that the folks in the driver's seat would need a map to find the steering wheel and said, "I'll take it from there."

"They hired me to write the bible. I left Walter's fine book alone, and instead, created *Two from Nowhere*, a pre-YA fantasy movie to become a regular week-to-week tv series. No one at that time had done what has, sadly today, become pro forma.

I had a young prince of coruscating light—old enough to absorb the wisdom of his elders, but not young enough to be as tragic as Shia LaBeouf: an idiot and a plagiarist. He comes with a major-domo, because every Mandrake the Magician needs his Lothar; everybody's gotta have a fall-back guy, somebody who can put a noose around the neck of the guy about to stab him.

"I said there will be a strong pro-survival, climate-aware feel to this; all of the things that the prince from Erehwon does will—in some way—have a salutary impact on this world, helping all the people thereon. The people who will get in his way are not evil. They're just human beings, and they're not thinking seven chess moves ahead; they're just serving their own needs and getting in the way. He'll never kill anybody. Occasionally, he'll have to bitch-slap somebody when their carelessness or stupidity gets in the way of logic."

Ellison wrote a detailed bible for the series, but ran for the hills during Development, which—in 1970s television—was generally when the suits tried to cram a *Two from Nowhere*-shaped idea into a *Fugitive*-shaped hole, beating it with the cudgels of banality until it fit. "That's all there was—characterizations, a little dialogue, suggested storylines—all of the moral and intellectual bases were in the bible."

"Very soon thereafter, out comes *The Powers of Matthew Star*. Boy, that sounds familiar. I called John Davies, attorney for Paramount, and I said 'John, I think they did it again. He didn't even ask who: 'How much you want?'"

## TWO FROM NOWHERE

Is the story of the exile and flight of two

remarkable "people."

KERT    an eleven-year-old boy who holds the

key to the universes

a child who stands between us and

the terrible forces of chaos

but he is only a child

GARDINEL    an old man, a wizard, a Merlin

steeped in fantastic wisdom

just a little wild, by normal

standards perhaps a mad old man

but he is the child's protector

Their story in just a moment.  But first...

TWO FROM NOWHERE

Rub your eyes and think of the world around you. The planet Earth stretching to the horizon, the night sky filled with other stars...other suns around which hurtle other earths called Proxima Centauri I and Alpha Omicron 5 and Denebola Lambda 88. And all the island universes that we see merely as sprinkles of chalk dust in the lens of the most powerful interstellar telescope.

Now forget it all.

Picture the universe as a box. And now see it inside a somewhat larger box. And that box inside an even larger box. Box after box, all occupying the same space, like a celestial nest of Chinese puzzle-boxes. Each one a complete universe of worlds and suns and people, separated only because each one vibrates at a different rate, each one invisible to all the others.

Right beside you, where you cannot see it, another world laid on top ours, and beside that one, membrane-thin, yet another, and another, on to the end of infinity.

Kept separate, kept apart, kept from leaking into each other by three incredible items:

The Unsleeping Eye

The Wand of Souls

The Golden Powerstone

ELLISON / 3

These three totems of power belong to the ruler of the next invisible universe to ours. Shall we call it Earth$_2$ or the Fourth Dimension or simply by its real name, the name used by the superior intelligence that rules it?

Call it EREWHON.

The hereditary rulers of Erewhon, through possession and benevolent use of the three focuses of power, and because of genetic refinements in their bloodline that give them special powers, have literally held together the tender fabric of space/time between the universes since time immemorial.

But CARDOL, the Father of the Universes is dying.

And the heir to the throne, his son KERT, is only eleven years old. Not yet strong enough or secure enough or wise enough in the use of his powers, to take the reins of power. His mentor and friend, the old wizard GARDINEL, will exercise a caretakership till Kert is of age, ten years hence.

How simple it seems.

Except for THONE.

Half-brother to Kert, only half as capable of using the blood-powers of the hereditary rulers, Thone is the pretender to the throne. He will have it, no matter what!

ELLISON / 4

Perhaps it should be understood that Kert, Gardinel, Thone, all of the "residents" of Erewhon are not human as we know the term. They are not "boys" or "men" or "rulers" as we envision such things.

They are light-energy creatures.

Living flames.

Shafts of coruscating light, as close to pure intellect as beings can be and still retain touch with physical presence. They know love and hate and pain and courage and friendship and compassion...perhaps more than human beings ...but they are not people.

Cardol, knowing he is bound for death--what those of Erewhon call dispersal--uses the last of his innate powers and places a force field around the three focuses of power. To be held inviolate until Kert can assume ownership, when the time has come that Gardinel feels he is wise enough and strong enough to rule Erewhon and capable enough to hold together the network web of space-time.

Cardol dies, his light dispersed.

But Thone has no intention of waiting for Kert to take his place. He moves to kill Kert.

Gardinel has known of Thone's intentions, has spoken to Cardol of it; and Kert's father has entrusted Kert's life to Gardinel. "Keep him safe till the day." They were Cardol's last words before dispersal.

An attempt is made on Kert's life-force, but Gardinel's alertness saves the boy. But it becomes clear there is no place in the world of Erewhon that is safe for Kert. But Gardinel, as clever as he is, does not know where to hide. There is no sanctuary safe from Thone and his legions.

What Gardinel does not know--because he has never needed to know it--and what even Cardol never suspected, is that Kert has much greater maturity than anyone knew. He steals into the Crystal Prism where the three focuses of power are kept, and he opens the force field.

"Father," the boy says, softly, to the empty air, "dear father, forgive me." And he takes The Unsleeping Eye that controls the gateways between universes.

Then, with Gardinel, with Thone close on their heels (though theyhave no heels...in fact, have no feet), they create a shimmering nimbus of translucency, and slip out of the world of Erewhon.

Remember the boxes within boxes...

(Some of the worlds are nexus points. They are more important than others. Just as New York, Los Angeles and Paris, London, Moscow and Rio de Janeiro are more important than Billings, Montana or Dayton, Ohio. Erewhon is a nexus world. So is the universe in which we live, the universe that contains the Earth.)

ELLISON / 6

Even as Thone mortally wounds Kert, the boy and the
old wizard slip through the created gateway between the
universes.  And Kert comes to Earth.

Two spears of rainbow light.

One a child with powers unknown to humans; a child who
holds the fate of all the universes in his hands; a child
who possesses The Unsleeping Eye that can foretell the future
and extrapolate ways in which it can be changed; but an
alien <u>child</u> nonetheless, exiled to a world so strange to him
that <u>nothing</u> is the same as on Erewhon.

The other an old man with wisdom beyond our wildest
dreams; a wizard with the power to change his physical
shape into anything he chooses; a cranky and mischievous
old wizard more prone to getting into trouble than the
child he guards; but a loving old man in a strange land,
nonetheless.

Light-beams, shape-changers, guardians of the web of
the universes, all that stand between us and chaos, Kert and
Gardinel leap through the gateway; the old wizard must keep
the young boy safe from Thone's attempts to kill him, for
a period of time that we measure here on Earth as "ten
years."

But Thone does not give up that easily.  Even though his
familial powers are half those of the pure-bred Kert, he

is a member of the ruling class and has sporadic, imperfect
control over the gateway between Earth and Erewhon. Though
he cannot open the gateway at random, though it costs him
dear each time he _does_ conjure it open, though he can only
send through one of his agents at a time...still, he _can_
do it. His long light _can_ reach through time and space to
pursue the exiled heir to the throne.

But even more, Thone can manipulate events in our
universe; to threaten the stability of our existence so that
Kert will be driven back from this sanctuary to Erewhon,
where Thone can get at him.

How does he manipulate events to make our universe
inhospitable for Kert?

For instance:

He causes to be born in the atmosphere of one small
town in the midwest, an unknown germ that kills as the
"Legionnaires Disease" did in Philadelphia. The town is
quarantined. Kert is in that town. All around him people
are becoming ill and falling toward coma, and he knows when
the time is right, one of the townspeople--a shape-changed
agent of Thone--will come for him.

Or:

The Unsleeping Eye warns Kert that in a way it cannot
yet perceive, Thone has reached through the gateway to

set in motion events that will cause a cataclysm on Earth.
He indicates the area of turbulence is in mid-California,
near Sacramento. Kert--knowing that he and Gardinel must
keep our universe stable or he must flee again--go to the
area. They discover, over the period of one segment, that
Thone, while unable to slip an actual agent across the
barrier from Erewhon, has implanted a corrupt thought in
the minds of several city planning commissioners that opens
them to corruption, bribes from a giant conglomerate that
seeks to build a paper mill over a dangerous fault running
into the San Andreas. The constant impact of the machines
will open the fault and set earthquake forces in motion
that will cause a disaster, thereby tearing the fabric of
our world a little more.

Or...

Well, that's the first story in the continuing flight
of this "little prince" and his wizard companion, and we'll
get to that later on. But first, here are a few more
elements of the background you should know.

Erewhon does not operate quite as the universe of Earth
does. Science does not work. Magic does. The laws of the
physical universe as we know them simply do not obtain in

ELLISON / 9

Erewhon. Like Oz, like Alice's Wonderland, like the hobbit world of Tolkien's Lord of the Rings, Erewhon is filled with creatures and abilities we consider myth and fantasy.

How strange it will be for Kert in our world of gravity and non-telepathic communication and animals that are simply animals. What happens the first time he needs to fly, and cannot? How does he feel when he finds he cannot speak from mind to mind with Gardinel? Will he become impaired, like a retarded child? Or will he adapt and learn how to seem to be a human being? In every sense, more completely than the lowliest orphan child on Earth, he is a stranger in a strange land, a complex and fascinating creature ripped suddenly from everything he has known as normality, and thrust into a strange new world where his conjuring powers are limited, where the simplest act of magic on Erewhon becomes a dangerous exercise here.

And what of Gardinel? He's an old man. How sad and lost will he become when he realizes his twilight years must be spent as a fugitive? Can his crazy sense of humor, his bemusement at these peculiar human beings, be brought under control? Or will he occasionally turn himself into a dragon that attacks a Chevy station wagon in a shopping center mall? And will his playful nature endanger Kert?

Understand something else: the creatures of Erewhon

exercise a highly-developed sense of personal ethics. (A very good thing for a young 8:00 audience to be exposed to.)

While they can go from ind to mind, even enter the bodies of other creatures, they refrain from doing so unless they have the agreement of the host intelligence, unless it is absolutely necessary, unless it has beneficial results. And so, though Kert and Gardinel <u>can</u> slip into someone's mind, they seldom do it. Temporary shared residence, perhaps, but never usurpation.

And, as we have seen, Kert <u>can</u> get through the force field Cardol set up around the three focuses of power. But he doesn't. Once, to save his life, he does it, to obtain The Unsleeping Eye and to get away from Erewhon. But not otherwise. Why? Because his father said not to do it till he was ready for such power.

Does this make Kert and Gardinel and the fantasy creatures of Erewhon better than human beings? Perhaps. It certainly makes them more interesting in some necessarily important ethical and moral ways. Ways that may serve as templates for our own world. Do we, perhaps, have a palatable way of demonstrating noble behavior to a contemporary television audience in the behavior of Kert and Gardinel...?

One would hope this aspect of the saga would be explored in depth each week.

ELLISON / 11

As for Thone, apart from his use as a mysterious Gray Eminence always waiting in the background, it should be apparent from the git-go that he is a creature more concerned with his own desires than with the fate of the universes. Consider: he cannot manipulate the powerful forces that hold together the fabric of space-time as well as Kert when he has reached maturity. He is an incomplete man, insensate with the need for power. If he has his way, if he disperses Kert and--with the death of Kert--manages to break the force field around The Wand of Souls and The Golden Powerstone, he will cause upheaval and disaster throughout the myriad worlds that link together at nexus points like Earth and Erewhon. He does not care. Thousands, perhaps millions of worlds will be destroyed, entire universes may cease to exist, uncountable intelligent races will die...Thone does not care. There will still be enough universes left for him to rule.

Like the devil, Thone's philosophy is "better to rule in Hell than to serve in Heaven."

A creature capable of such destruction does not pause for an instant in wreaking havoc to such a puny battlefield as Earth, nor does the death of his younger half-brother distress him in the slightest. Thone, clearly, is one of the great demon figures. Evil, but fascinating. And dangerous.

And what of The Unsleeping Eye?

Though Kert possesses it, the very ownership of this incredibly potent totem of power has its drawbacks. Where can he hide it? Must he carry it with him at all times? How can he ever feel safe and secure here on Earth when the Eye constantly apprises him of new problems created by Thone, problems Kert must set to rights or lose the universe of the Earth? And, like all magical icons, it has its own life-force. It has arcane needs that Kert and Gardinel must satisfy or the Eye itself can become a danger to them. Its presence in our world, a thing of necromancy, is an alien force itself. It is a serious responsibility for an eleven year old child in a strange world.

Not to mention The Golden Powerstone that contains within its matrix the unnameable forces that hold together the fabric of space-time...and The Wand of Souls that can tap into the lives of every living thing in all the universes. These two items, left behind, exert a tremendous call on Kert. He cannot simply run away, close off the gateway and never return to Erewhon. The Wand and the Powerstone are still there. Though he does not physically possess them now, they represent the enormity of the legacy his father left behind. Responsibility...another important aspect of this story. The debts we owe others, the need to fulfill our destiny, the duty to others that makes us strong, the accountability for our acts. In Kert, and his sense of responsibility we see a paradigm of our own lives.

And don't forget, he's still young. So he learns. As Gardinel teaches (all the while learning about Earth himself), Kert becomes a young adult. A child, lost and with only one person he can trust, he stumbles and makes mistakes, but becomes strong and wise. This is a story of growing up. Like <u>Penrod</u> and <u>Huckleberry Finn</u>, like <u>Catcher in the Rye</u> and most especially like <u>The Once and Future King</u>, this is an ongoing study of childhood melding into maturity, of innocence being informed by experience, of the emergence of a caring, intelligent individual.

But there are surprises to come even at this stage of the explication of Kert and Gardinel's exile.

I've saved them till now because I hope they will form the crux of the pilot segment of this series.

So let us leap through the gateway opened by The Unsleeping Eye and follow Kert and Gardinel to the Earth...

From Erewhon which, if you rearrange the letters, is an anagram for Nowhere.

Leap through the magic gateway with these two...

TWO FROM NOWHERE.

ELLISON / 14

TWO FROM NOWHERE

The Beginning

An alley in a nameless city.  Night in a nameless
American city.  And those without home prowl.

Dimly, through the darkness, we see a man in the
process of mugging a small boy.  Who the boy may be, and
who the man may be...we do not know.  We may never know.
But it is yet another senseless act of urban brutality.

As the man cuffs the boy around, at the far end of the
filthy alley, among the crates and garbage cans, we suddenly
see a fantastic choreography of light and electrical
radiation.  The mugger and the child do not see what is
happening behind them.

The glow waxes and wavers and wanes and a multi-colored,
prismatic orchestration of otherworldly strangeness grows
in the darkness, covering everything with strange colors
and strobing eerieness.  Then the glow becomes the eye of
some alien creature, like the many-faceted eye of a bee,

in which we see, repeated a thousand times over, the sight
of two beams of light streaking toward us, getting larger in
each facet of the eye. Behind them a dark, blood-red beam
of light pursues. There is an instant of violence as the
red beam of light spurts a flame-like tongue at the smaller
of the two fleeing golden lights, and then the huge glow
in the alley irises and the two beams of golden light
streak through an materialize in the alley.

The gateway closes quickly, leaving the two beams of
light pulsing at the end of the alley in darkness as the
mugger hits the boy and sends him down.

We HEAR IN ECHO OVER the "voices" of Kert and Gardinel.

> GARDINEL
> You are hurt, my Prince.

> KERT
> Thone...he...tried to disperse me.

> GARDINEL
> I sense your essence is failing.

> KERT
> We need shelter, Gardinel.
> (beat)
> That child. The man has hurt him.
> He's dying. Quickly, Gardinel!

The smaller beam of golden light arcs up and over and
shoots toward the unconscious child. It reaches him, bathes
him in a golden glow, and then they are one.

The larger beam of golden light races toward the mugger,
who stands with a brick, ready to hit the child again.

                        GARDINEL
            Please excuse me, but I cannot permit
            you to continue being violent.

And the golden beam of light washes over the drunken

mugger, the man stands bathed in the glow, the light pulses

as though there is a struggle taking place, and then they

are one.  The mugger's eyes glaze and he freezes in mid-step.

CAMERA COMES IN QUICKLY on the unconscious face of the

eleven year old boy into which the essence of Kert has gone.

We HEAR OVER the interior dialogue...in two distinct voices.

                        KERT
            Boy, forgive me for entering your
            mind without permission.

                        CHARLIE
                    (faintly)
            What happened...?

                        KERT
            The man.  He hurt you.  I think
            you are dispersing...dying.

                        CHARLIE
            I'm afraid.

                        KERT
            Dispersal is frightening.  I've
            been told.

                        CHARLIE
            Who are you?

                        KERT
            Kert, prince of Erewhon.  I came
            into you because I have been hurt
            also.  Please excuse my intrusion.

                        CHARLIE
            Sure...it's okay...I feel like I'm
            going away...
                                    (CONTINUED:)

ELLISON / 17

                        KERT
Boy?  How are you called?

                        CHARLIE
Charlie.

                        KERT
What made the man hurt you?

                        CHARLIE
                    (crying)
I don't know.  I didn't do nothing
to him.  I just ran away from the
Home and I was comin' down the
street...I think he was drunk...

                        KERT
Much of what you say has no meaning
for me.

                        CHARLIE
I feel so funny...like I was slipping
off somewhere...

                        KERT
You are dispersing.
                    (beat)
Boy...Charlie...when you are gone...
forgive my asking but I must...may I
use your shell to contain my essence?

                        CHARLIE
I don't know...what...you...mean...

                        KERT
I am hurt.  Exposed, in my natural
state, I will disperse.  Contained here
in your shell, I can live.  May I?

                        CHARLIE
I guess that'd mean I'd still keep
on living...in a way...wouldn't I?

                        KERT
Yes, friend.

                        CHARLIE
                    (very faintly)
Okay.  It's yours...Kert...
                    (fading)
Kert...I'm going...away...goodbye...

                            (CONTINUED:)

ELLISON / 18

                    KERT
                 (sadly)
          Goodbye, Charlie friend. I will
          take very good care of your shell.
          Thank you...


But Gardinel is having some trouble inside <u>his</u> human

sanctuary. The mugger is inside there with them, they're

like The Odd Couple, both inhabiting a very small apartment.


                    GUMBO
          Yoick! What's happening? I feel
          awful.

                    GARDINEL
          No wonder, you terrible person. Your
          system is filled with poison.

                    GUMBO
          That's the best muscatel a dollar can
          buy!

                    GARDINEL
          A dollar. I perceive that to be a
          measure of currency, a rate of exchange.
                 (beat)
          You have taken another's life for a
          dollar? How can you bear to live with
          yourself in this shell?

                    GUMBO
          I don't know what you're talking about.
          Get outta here and lemme alone, you
          creep!

                    GARDINEL
          I amextremely sorry I have invaded your
          shell, man, but I cannot permit you to
          do more harm. But I will make myself
          useful by excising the poison from your
          system.

The body of the mugger glows a bright blue.

                    GUMBO
          Hey! I'm not drunk no more.

                              (CONTINUED:)

ELLISON / 19

>                    GARDINEL
>     You have done your shell considerable
>     damage.  It is a slovenly place to
>     live.
>
>                    GUMBO
>     You talk about it like it was a room
>     in a flophouse.
>
>                    GARDINEL
>     Now that you are clear in yourself,
>     can you perceive what you have done?
>
>                    GUMBO
>                  (terrified)
>     Oh my God.  I hurt that little kid.
>     I--I didn't know what I was doing.
>     I was bagged.  Oh, God...

The mugger, GUMBO, permits Gardinel to stay within

him for a while, till he can establish communications with

Kert.

They decide that Kert will remain in the body of the

dead Charlie.  But that is an empty shell.  It is ethically

acceptable.  Gardinel's staying inside Gumbo cannot be

tolerated.  The wizard prepares to vacate the premises,

but Gumbo has been thinking.  He asks Gardinel if he would

stay on a while...straighten him out...correct the bent

and twisted things in Gumbo's mind that made him the

derelict he is.  Kert and Gardinel discuss it and decide

if Gumbo wants to allow the wizard to stay in there with

him, it will be advantageous.  But only for a while.  In

exchange for straightening Gumbo out, the mugger will offer

ELLISON / 20

temporary shelter.

(It goes without saying that Gumbo does not understand
that Gardinel and Kert are light-energy creatures from another
time-universe.  He only knows that for the first time in
many years he feels like a human being.)

Gardinel agrees to take on the job of making Gumbo a
human being but insists that when he has done the job, Gumbo
will turn himself in for what he did to Charlie.  The deal
is struck.

And so Kert and the wizard have human form.  Now they
must begin to discover how their new world functions, and
they must set up a way of life for themselves that Thone
cannot penetrate.

And so begins their journey through our world.

NOTE: This part of the story is imperative to show in the
       first segment of the series.  Unlike the readily
acceptable templates of cop, western, doctor or contemporary
situation comedy shows, we are building a fantasy construct
that must be rigorously and logically established.  Unlike
virtually any other mimetic presentation, a make-believe
world must be set out and set up carefully so the audience
is well oriented from the start.

ELLISON / 21

## TWO FROM NOWHERE

### The First Story

Time is spent learning how to live in bodies.  The
laws of the physical universe are discovered, with often
amazing results...some funny...others frightening...

For instance:

Gardinel grows weak and falls down.  Gumbo points
out that with the exception of some cheap wine, he hasn't
eaten in almost five days.  Then they have to explain
"eating" to one another.  For light-energy beings, merely
being exposed to the rays of the sun are food enough.  So
Gardinel has to discover food.  He learns to hate beets
and boiled carrots, but comes to love kumquats and hot
dogs.

When Gardinel sees his first automobile with a woman
driving it, he assumes it's a fierce beast that has swallowed
a person, and changes into a mammoth animal that snorts
and butts the car.  He is trying to be chivalrous, to save
the woman.  It takes a while to straighten that one out.

Kert tries to talk telepathically to a dog, to ask directions. The dog howls at the attempted intrusion and runs away. Gumbo explains, through Gardinel, that animals don't talk on Earth.

Kert has to learn how to keep his body going. He is still just a light-energy creature, symbiotically sharing the shell of a dead and gone Charlie, and when he cuts himself and doesn't stop bleeding, observers get panicky, until Gumbo tells Gardinel that Kert has to make himself clot. Gardinel tells the onlookers the boy is a hemophiliac and they cover the gaffe in that way till they can get away.

But finally, they are comfortable in their shells, and though Gardinel keeps having a running argument with Gumbo about ethics, about the world, about how to do this or that, which direction to take, they begin to wander through the country.

They are in a small midwestern town when The Unsleeping Eye begins to clow and pulse with an inner heat that is almost painful when Kert holds the mysterious orb in his hand.

With a strange, sepulchural voice, the Eye tells them that in this town Thone is making a move against the Earth and against them. The Eye cannot yet extrapolate the nature of the threat, but its sensing abilities tell it that it has something to do with a young boy on a bike who passes them. The boy is KENNY DORMAN and he is working his paper route. Kert and Gardinel are assured by the Eye that if they do not intercede and thwart Thone in this unexplicated maneuver, it can have serious repercussions. The Eye says that as time passes, and matters develop, it will be able to give them more clues to the nature of the problem.

Kert meets Kenny. The newsboy asks Kert what his name is, and when Kert starts to say his name he realizes he must pay homage to the person who lived in this shell before him. He tells Kenny his name is Charlie Kert. He introduces the wizard as his uncle, Gardy.

Kert says they've just come to town and asks where a good place to live might be. Kenny suggests a rooming house on his route. Kert wants to know if it's possible for himself to get a paper route, to make some money.

(Both Kert and Gardinel really have no trouble with money. When they need some, Gardinel just conjures it up using a handful of fallen leaves as substance from which to draw form.)

Kenny says he'd be glad to help Charlie get a route. And he does. In this way, by following along with Kenny on his route, Kert is able to keep tabs on him. Both Kert and Gardinel wait expectantly for Thone's plan to materialize.

Kert finds Kenny's mind fascinating.  The boy has a
highly developed sense of fantasy and when he talks to
Kert about the world around them, he sees it in ways that
Kert finds difficult to interpret.  For instance...

"You know how highways get here?" Kenny says to
Kert one afternoon.

"I suppose they're built by people with machines,"
Kert answers.  But he isn't sure.  This is a new world for
him, remember?

"Uh-uh," says Kenny, grinning.  "The way it happens
is this: there's a big pink worm, about a hundred feet around,
see, and it goes slurpin' and slitherin' through the world,
all the way around the world.  And where it passes, it leaves
this sticky trail of stuff that hardens and becomes highways."

When Kert realizes Kenny is just daydreaming this wild
invention, he starts laughing.  On Erewhon they have very
good sense of humor.  "Well, then," Kert asks, "who paints
the lines down the middle?"

Kenny is pleased that Kert has joined in his little
game.  He starts laughing and says, "Oh, that's easy.  Very
tiny men with long noses that end in paintbrushes come in
the dead of the night and paint the lines on the worm track."

"They must have perfect balance," Kert says.  They never
make the lines wiggle."

But Kert discovers that others do not share his pleasure and fascination with Kenny's wild way of seeing the universe. They don't understand him, and he constantly gets in trouble as a result of his misinterpretations of what adults want, what they believe.

And as Kert and Kenny become friends, we see two very different (yet very much alike) entities coming to grips with the way the world has of killing dreams, of limiting imagination in the young.

Kert, as Charlie, camps out one night in Kenny's backyard. And in the night, Kert is able to barely touch Kenny's sleeping mind with his own. He does not enter Kenny's mind, but permits Kenny's sleeping thoughts to penetrate his own thinking. And Kenny **sees** Erewhon. It is a sensational guided tour for a young boy. And when he wakes up, he tells Kert what he "dreamed." Kert tells him there may be a world like that somewhere, that he should keep thinking about far places and strange lands.

Slowly, however, Thone's plan becomes known to The Unsleeping Eye. It is complex and terrible, and only a magic orb from another universe could perceive the awful steps that lead Thone's plan to end in tragedy.

It is like an evil game of dominoes. Here are the steps:

ELLISON / 26

There is a United States Senator who holds the swing vote on a military appropriations bill.

If the bill passes, it will escalate the potentiality for a new war in which the United States would be involved, because of the upgraded sophistication of armaments.

The Senator's Executive Assistant has the information to prepare a report to the Senator that will convince him he should vote no on the bill.

He has not yet prepared the report.

He has come home to his family for a brief rest from the turmoil of Washington, and to have the quiet time to think and prepare the report, to be delivered when he goes back in a week.

Every day at a certain time, Kenny Dorman pedals down the street on which the Senator's Assistant's parents live.

Every day at the same time, a delivery truck passes down the next street parallel to the street Kenny uses on his route.

On the day after tomorrow, instead of taking the usual street of its route, the delivery truck driver will receive a blinding stab of pain, a sharp short burst of a headache, and he will turn down the street Kenny uses. He will come toward the boy approaching on his bicycle just as a young man in a three-piece suit emerges from a house and starts to cross the street.

At that moment the delivery van driver will receive a second crushing pain. The first sent him down the wrong street, the second will make him swerve and head directly toward the boy on the bicycle.

The man in the three-piece suit will see the truck about to hit the boy, and he will jump out just as the bike passes him, and hurl the boy safely out of the path of danger.

The truck will kill the man in the three-piece suit.

The negative report to the Senator will not be written.

The Senator will vote aye on the bill.

And war will result, in less than a year.


All this the unbelievable arcane orb, THE UNSLEEPING EYE, tells Kert and Gardinel.

All this, but slowly, in bits and pieces as Thone works at the peak of his incomplete, imperfect powers, to open a gateway just wide enough, just long enough, to fire a mental power bolt at the driver of the delivery van. Two short bursts, only a second or two in duration, but the key two seconds to start a worldwide conflagration that will so unravel the stability of the Earth universe that Kert and Gardinel would be forced to flee back to Erewhon.

And because it is a living organism itself, The Unsleeping
Eye takes its time in telling them what they need to know.
At one final point, as time grows terribly short, Gardinel
has had enough and a wild verbal battle ensues between
the wizard in the body of the mugger, and the beautiful
glowing Eye.  Some people might think the argument funny.

They discover the plan, and they take steps to keep
Kenny off the street at that time.

But things go wrong.

Kenny is there, as destiny has ordered, and so is the
Senator's Assistant, and so is the driver of the delivery
van...with a blinding pain in his head.

But so, too, are Kert and Gardinel.

They think they can use their powers to stop the tragedy.
To change Gardinel into a tree trunk fallen across the road,
to blow out Kenny's tire, to make the Assistant stumble.
But at the penultimate moment they realize Thone has been
even too devious for The Unsleeping Eye.  It was all a ruse,
the complex plot about the Senator's Assistant.

The targets of the truck are Kert and Gardinel, lured
to this spot, at this moment, by a Machiavellian Thone who
has known they would use the orb to pierce his plan.

The truck swerves toward Kert and Gardinel rushing
toward the Assistant, and at the last moment Kenny sees
what is happening, and pedals furiously alongside the truck,

screaming at the driver. He swerves back at the last moment, but hits Kenny on his bike.

The truck stops, Kenny has been thrown across the street, lies unconscious, and the Senator's Assistant and Kert and Gardinel rush to him. They're joined by the truck driver.

The boy is unconscious.

While Kert goes for Kenny's parents, Gardinel and the Assistant get Kenny into the rear of the delivery van and rush him to the hospital.

They operate. Kenny is blind.

Seemingly, it is a tragedy without hope. But in the night Kert has Gardinel leave Gumbo's body and come with him to the hospital. Gardinel changes himself into a rat and scampers around the nurse's station so Kert can sneak past to Kenny's room.

Once there, Kert talks to the boy, tells him that even if he cannot see the world around him, there are still all the worlds of his imagination, that he can be a writer of fantasies, can make _others_ see the universe as an endless series of Chinese puzzle boxes within boxes within boxes.

And then he joins minds with Kenny and shows him the dream world of Erewhon again. Except this time, Kenny is awake.

"Who are you, Charlie?" Kenny asks. Kert takes his

hands and holds them as he says, "I'm someone just like
you, Kenny. I'm all alone in a dark place, trying to
make it as nice as I can till it gets light again." And
he promises Kenny that there are other times, other worlds,
other universes where eyes don't work the way they do on
Earth; where Kenny will be able to see again, but see in
different ways...see colors that sing...and wind that
flows like a river through azure skies...where the people
are only light beams and the dreams he can have there are
free of misunderstanding.

Kenny says he'll think about such places, and Kert
assures him that the mental touches they've shared will
not dim. Inside his blind eyes, Kenny has a living world
of wonder far more supportable than the real world of
limited adults who have lost their inner vision.

They part, with Kert giving Kenny a gift far more
valuable than the one stolen from him by Thone.

And now they must move on, Kert and Gardinel.

Thone can locate them if they stay at that focus of
his gateway.

Will Gardinel go back into Gumbo's body, share that
dumpy apartment body with the reformable mugger? Or will
he become a dog, an automobile, a cabretta-grain attache
case, a katydid?

Will Kert learn from his experiences and grow in
wisdom? Will he become the sort of adult who can hold

ELLISON / 31

the enormous power Cardol bequeathed him, control the
terrible forces that link the universes together, stave
off chaos?  Can he stay out of the jaws of Thone long
enough to regain the throne of Erewhon?

Only time, week by week, adventure by adventure,
will tell.  But there's no one else telling this kind
of adventure, and so all the world, all the myriad worlds,
stretch before Kert, the little Prince of Erewhon, and
Gardinel, his personal Merlin...

TWO FROM NOWHERE.

AND NOW, TO

DEMONSTRATE THE SCOPE OF

THIS SERIES, SOME RANDOM

STORY SPRINGBOARDS...

ELLISON / 32

### two from nowhere

### STORY SPRINGBOARDS

1.  Gardinel falls in love.  This crazy old wizard, more
    prone to playing magical practical jokes than ever to
settling down in an ivy-covered cottage, gets pierced by
Cupid's arrows and takes up with a widow lady.  What are
the chances of the wise old man's paying any attention
when Kert tells him he thinks the woman is one of Thone's
agents in an invaded body?  Would you listen to an eleven
year old child who told you the person you love is a
demon in disguise?

2.  Gumbo was wanted by the police.  He is caught, and
    so is Gardinel.  Can the wizard desert the man who
has willingly sheltered him, who is on the road to moral
recovery, merely to save himself?  And what will the
authorities do with a child who has no guardian?  The
holder of the power to rule the universes...in an
orphanage?

3.  Foolish and bored, a group of urban swinging singles

has been playing at black magic, summoning up the devil,
silly black masses as excuses for partner-swapping and
other sophomoric activities. But when Gardinel and Kert
come to live at one of their homes--Gardinel working as
a handyman--real magic begins to work. And then the games
get a bit more rugged.


4. Who was Charlie? Why did he run away from "the Home"?
    What was he doing in that alley? Has he parents? Was
he an orphan? Could something terrible have happened that
forced Charlie to run off? And what if someone is looking
for him because, perhaps, he saw something he shouldn't
have seen? The moment presents itself when a woman rushes
up to Kert on the street and throws her arms around him.
Who is it? It's Charlie's mother.


5. Thone has reached through from the gateway and lured
    Gardinel out of the body he was occupying...perhaps
it's still Gumbo's. And Thone has made sure the old
wizard can't get back into another. Kert must leave the
shell of Charlie to save him, but more than a few moments
out of that human sanctuary and the child will die. Has
Kert learned enough about self-sacrifice to risk death?

A FEW LAST WORDS ABOUT

TWO FROM NOWHERE

Anywhere. That's where these stories can go. Not just in three dimensions, here and there from the locales used for every other television series, but in four, five, ten, a hundred dimensions. Back to Erewhon. Into the future. Into the past. Into other dimensions. Into the human heart and obviously into the imagination.

Kert is The Little Prince...a charmer, yet strong and growing with each episode. Gardinel is comic, but wise and caring; in his own cockeyed way responsible in the extreme. He is Merlin with a lampshade on his head.

If there isn't an audience for fresh, innovative fantasy like this, then we might as well give up television to the used car salesmen.

I offer this special dream with care and affection.

                                    HARLAN ELLISON
                                    1 November 76

ELLISON / 1

PLEASE NOTE

At least one-half of any pilot script written as the
initial segment of TWO FROM NOWHERE must include the
fantasy backstory of Kert and Gardinel (as set forth
in the presentation, 1 Nov 76), modified and altered
as per subsequent discussions to fit the new parameters
of the continuing story-line.

These story springboards are constructed to fill no
more than two acts, with the understanding that as
each story unfolds, the backstory and basic tenets
of the series will be concurently revealed.  Thus,
each segment as presented here will have two major
threads running simultaneously.

These are intended as samples of typical kinds of
stories, with the hope that no immutable template
will be chosen, that flexibility and fluidity of
direction will be permitted.

HARLAN ELLISON

ELLISON / 2

## STORY #1

Kert and Gardinel try to set up new identities in a small
midwestern town where a bitter struggle is being waged
between business interests desiring to set up a mini
steel mill in an otherwise rustic area, and the wholly
responsible, non-rabid environmentalist elements who
point out that it is Japanese industrial money that is
behind the plan, brought to their small town because the
pollution conditions in Japan are so serious they cannot
construct the plant there. The waste from scrap metal
and junked car bodies used to make ingots for shipping
back to Japan would ruin their town.

## STORY #2

A divorced man, denied access to his daughter, a small
child, goes a little crazy and kidnaps the child. He
takes hostages to protect him while he gets away with
the little girl. Kert is one of the hostages. This
would be a story along the lines of "Sugarland Express"
with compassion and not violence as the keynote.

ELLISON / 3

## STORY #3

A "closed circle" story that takes place in an old, extensive
Southern mansion, abandoned years before. Kert and Gardinel
stop overnight while on the road, and find that Thone has
reached through from Erewhon and put a force field around
the house. They cannot get out, and are stalked through
its many rooms and subterranean passages (left over from
the Civil War days of the Underground Railroad) by one of
Thone's agents. This seems an ideal story, because it
provides present danger and action, while providing respite
time to explore the backstory in flashback. An additional
element would be an old man, half-deluded into thinking
he's the last survivor of the Civil War, who has been
living in the walls of the house for many years. Echos
of the last island survivor of WWII who recently was
discovered in the jungles of some Pacific atoll.

## STORY #4

A "disaster" story in which Kert and Gardinel find themselves
saving lives during a major fire that breaks out in a
border town between Texas and Mexico. In this story,
Kert has to give up one of his major powers--the inability
to feel pain--to save other people's lives. By giving up
this power he becomes more human, and thus gets to "know
his subjects" (as his father wished) more completely than
he could as a creature without the capacity to know pain.

Gnomebody

&

Love Amid the Ruins

## Editor's Note: Between a Brennert and an O'Bannon

"Gnomebody" first saw print in the October 1956 issue of *Amazing Stories*. The short story was subsequently collected in 1962's ELLISON WONDERLAND before bubbling to the surface of Ellison's mind while he was serving as creative consultant on CBS's 1985 incarnation of *The Twilight Zone*. "'Gnomebody' was a very simple fantasy gag with very little special effects—only one, as it turned out," recalled Ellison. "I could have thought up fifty-two ideas on the spot—'Gnomebody' or 'Rain, Rain Go Away'—there's any number of short-short stories that I've done as fillers for myself where, at the end of a long day of work, I thought 'I'm gonna do a quick short story' and I'd do a 1,500- to 2,000-word story—about eight pages, double-spaced—and that one came to mind; it's as random as that."

The 1985–1987 incarnation of the *Zone* took Rod Serling's anthology approach to the next level by presenting—within an hour-long timeslot—two or preferably three stories of varying length and complexity. At seven pages, Ellison's 22 March 1985 teleplay for "Gnomebody" would likely have bridged two lengthier stories. Why the script—written long before Ellison's 26 November 1985 resignation over "The Deadly 'Nackles' Affair" (which can be found, in all its gory detail, in his 1997 collection SLIPPAGE)—was never produced is a mystery to Ellison, who didn't even remember adapting the story until it was exhumed for this publication.

"Had I stayed with *Twilight Zone* longer, there were a lot more stories I was gonna do," laments Ellison. "One of them was about a haunted robot; I came across a piece of that story the other day." Another tale, titled "Love Amid the Ruins"—tangentially related to his *Logan's Run* story "Crypt" (in BRAIN MOVIES, Volume 5)—was submitted to the syndicated, Canadian-produced *Twilight Zone* follow-up alongside "Crazy as a Soup Sandwich" (in BRAIN MOVIES, Volume 1) but likewise remained unproduced, though Ellison recently moved his notes for the tale on to his To-Do stack.

"It was the greatest television time of my experience, working on *The Twilight Zone*, with Alan Brennert, Rockne O'Bannon, Phil DeGuere, Jim Crocker, Patrice Messina and myself as the story unit. We were a muscle—a gestalt—that it was a joy working with."

FADE IN:

1    EXT. JR. HIGH SCHOOL ATHLETIC FIELD - DAY

MEASURE - BG has the look of a 1940's film, obviously a matte or rearscreen projection. In FG the athletic coach, MR. ROLLIE, mid-forties, a little sloppy in the gut, cranky and fast-talking, argues with a fourteen-year-old kid, LOUIS GALLIGAN. Louis is in street garb, though the kids in the b.g. are in running gear, doing laps around the track.

> ROLLIE
> (fast & furious)
> Forget it, Galligan. Read my lips.
> N. O. In most parts of the world
> that passes for a dismissal.

> LOUIS
> (snotty)
> Hey, Mr. Rollie, that ain't good
> enough. Whyn't'cha gimme a <u>chance</u>
> at least?

> ROLLIE
> (inserting a stick
> of gum in his face)
> Because, Galligan, you are no-price.
> You haven't got the goods. You can't
> run. You're too slow. You're just
> <u>not</u> <u>fast</u>. I'm working on my third
> ulcer this year and <u>I'm</u> faster than
> you. My <u>Granny</u> is faster than you...
> and she's been dead since 1953.

> LOUIS
> Aw, c'mon, Mr. Rollie. I can run...
> gimme a <u>chance</u>!

> ROLLIE
> What I'll give you is the permanent
> mark of my cloven hoof on your butt
> if you don't get out of my face!

Louis gives him a hurt, sullen, adolescent drop-dead look, and storms off, hands deep in jeans pockets. Rollie shakes his head wearily, jams another stick of gum in his mouth, and turns away as we

                       CUT TO:

2    THE WOODS - DAY

CAMERA MOVES BETWEEN TREES in a deep, dark, tulgey wood.
We HEAR the SOUND of something heavy hitting a tree
trunk, and we HEAR Louis cursing and howling in an
inarticulate melange of sounds. Bam. Wham. Smesh!

CAMERA COMES THRU the thick foliage to reveal Louis with
a stout tree limb, bashing the hell out of a big oak or
similar creature. His cursing is gibberish.

                    LOUIS
                (inarticulate)
        Rassafrassen pecalomer...lousy mizrabble
        eggsuckin' crassbalin creeble!
                (etcetera)

CAMERA IN CLOSER as Louis lays a good one on the bole.
A strident VOICE O.S. rings out.

                    ISHMAEL O.S.
                (angrily)
        Put a sock in it, willya!?!

Louis is in mid-swing as the VOICE BOOMS.  So he slugs
the tree once more, inadvertently.  Boom!

                    ISHMAEL O.S.
                (ominously)
        You wanna go through life with an extra
        set of elbows, you little crud?

Louis, still holding the limb, walks around to the other
side of the tree.  CAMERA GOES WITH as the other side of
the tree comes into view.

3    THE TREE - THE HONEY HOLE

MEDIUM CLOSE on a perfectly round, fairly largeish, sorta
porthole-sized honey hole. Dark in there. Louis comes
into frame, looks around, sees nothing, looks at the hole.
Suddenly a face, neck, head and shoulders appear in the
honey hole. It is a gnome. We're talking walnut skinned,
bright green-eyed, tufted haired, wide-lipped gnome.

                    LOUIS
                (taken aback)
        Whaaaaah...!

                                    (CONTINUED:)

3    CONTINUED:

The gnome shoulder suddenly has a gnome arm and hand attached to it, and then the other, and both hands go to the gnome ears as Louis rends the air with his shriek.

                    ISHMAEL
          Quiet!  Silence!  Cease!  A pox on your
          throat, you bawling, blasphemous,
          incharitable dog!

Louis stares.  Mouth open.

                    ISHMAEL
                 (now warily)
          Whaddaya starin' at?

                    LOUIS
          You're a gnome.

                    ISHMAEL
                 (fastfastfast)
          No, I'm not.

                    LOUIS
          You are, too.

                    ISHMAEL
          I'm tellin' you I'm not!

                    LOUIS
          I know a gnome when I see one.

                    ISHMAEL
          Nothing like it.  I'm just a little
          person.

                    LOUIS
                 (strident)
          You live in a tree.  Little persons
          don't live in trees; gnomes live in
          trees.

                    ISHMAEL
          I couldn't get an apartment, I like
          the open air.

                    LOUIS
          Gnome.

                    ISHMAEL
                 (resigned)
          Well, y'found me out.

                              (CONTINUED:)

3     CONTINUED: - 2

                              LOUIS
                         (after a beat)
               You got a name they call ya?

                              ISHMAEL
               You couldn't pronounce it.

                              LOUIS
                         (narrowly)
               That a chop, mister?

                              ISHMAEL
                         (eyes to heaven)
               So call me Ishmael.

Louis stares at him a long beat.

                              LOUIS
               I'm gonna sell you to a teevee show.
               "That's Incredible." "Believe it or
               Not". "Freaks of the World." I'm
               gonna be rich.

                              ISHMAEL
                         (affronted)
               What a chunk of mud! What a drip of
               goo! Didn't your mother ever tell
               you it's not nice to sell people as
               if they were bruised fruit?
                         (beat)
               Mud! Goo! A stone, a rock, that's
               what you got for a heart.

                              LOUIS
               You're not a people. You're a gnome.
               I know all about your kind.

                              ISHMAEL
                         (offended)
               "Your kind"..."your kind..."?
               What sort of a reference is <u>that</u>, may
               I ask? Mud, goo, a stone: and a
               bigot, to boot!

                              LOUIS
                         (cagey)
               So give me the pot of gold and I
               won't sell you to teevee.

                                        (CONTINUED:)

3    CONTINUED: - 3

> ISHMAEL
> Sure. Naturally. Of course: this
> goo, this mud, this stone: a product
> of his times. Venal. Greedy.
> Upwardly mobile.

> LOUIS
> So you got the gold, gnome?

> ISHMAEL
> I don't do that one.

> LOUIS
> Which one?

> ISHMAEL
> Gold. I don't do gold. Also I don't
> do silver, rhodium, uranium or large
> amounts of tin.

> LOUIS
> So what do you do?

> ISHMAEL
> I do one wish.

> LOUIS
> I thought it was supposed to be three.

> ISHMAEL
> Times is tough. Sue me.
> (beat)
> One wish, anything you want.

> LOUIS
> Anything?

> ISHMAEL
> (exasperated)
> What is it with you? Do I stutter or
> something? I'm beginning to think
> human speech is not your natural tongue.

> LOUIS
> Okay, I'll take a wish.

> ISHMAEL
> What'll it be? Vast power? Immortality?
> How about the slavish adoration of cheap
> but sensual women?

(CONTINUED:)

3     CONTINUED: - 4

Louis is outraged, hands on hips.

> LOUIS
> (affronted)
> I'm fourteen years old, fer pete's sake!
> What's'a'matter with you?  What'm I gonna do
> with women?

> ISHMAEL
> Just a thought.  So what'll it be?

> LOUIS
> Lemme think a minute.

> ISHMAEL
> Then you go away and leave me in peace,
> right?

> LOUIS
> (abstracted)
> I'm thinking.

> ISHMAEL
> (aside)
> Moss is gonna grow on your north
> side first.

Louis snaps his fingers.

> LOUIS
> I got it!

> ISHMAEL
> (bored)
> I tremble at the promise of brilliance.

> LOUIS
> Make me so's I can run faster than
> anyone!

> ISHMAEL
> (crosses his eyes,
>   makes arcane
>   gestures)
> Zaka-doola-makka-doola.
> (beat)
> Done.
> (beat)
> Goodbye.

And POOF! he's gone.  CAMERA HOLDS ON LOUIS'S AMAZED
FACE as we:

> SMASH-cut to;

4    EXACTLY THE SAME AS SCENE 1

Rollie and Louis, in CLOSE so all we see are their faces
close to each other.

> ROLLIE
> I don't care, Galligan, you don't
> run for this school. No way, no
> chance, no time, not <u>never</u>!
> (beat, he gives
> him a sneer look)
> Whatta weirdo.

And he walks away as CAMERA PULLS BACK SLOWLY to show us
the sad-faced, miserable Louis Galligan who stands there
staring after the coach. Louis is a <u>centaur</u>. From the
waist up he is a fourteen-year-old schoolboy wearing a
t-shirt. From the waist down he is a horse.

CAMERA BACK as Louis stands there. Slowly he paws the
ground in cadence:

> LOUIS
> (paws, counts)
> One...two...three...

FADE TO BLACK

and

FADE OUT.

## LOVE AMID THE RUINS

Sixty-five years after an unnamed super-power has sown an airborne plague in the atmosphere. They were losing the War, and it was an act of madness. The plague decimated the Earth's population. It brought the War to an end...it ended all wars on the Earth. Now, sixty-five years later, he comes out of the rubble, seeking the last cryonic crypts in which the plague-carrying survivors were frozen in deep sleep, in hopes there would come a day when a cure could be found for them.

He comes seeking those crypts. He is a finalizer.

Science has found no cure for the plague. But like measles --once a great destroyer--the plague has died out. Those few who were immune have given birth to children whose systems resist the dread disease. Humanity, for the first time fully at peace, is courageously and steadily coming back. The only remaining threat is the few thousand sleeping in their pod support-tanks. If they are revived, they can wipe out a world just getting back on its feet. And so, the survivors have made a hard decision.

They have sent out this man--and others like him--who walks the land, using old records that pinpoint the crypts, doing the terrible deed of smashing the life-support systems, letting the plague-carriers sleep on into death.

It is a frightful responsibility, so only the most humane and committed have been selected as <u>finalizers</u>.

As we open, he comes out of the rubble on a hillside, studying the map. He is a tall, tanned man, rugged and decent-looking. In another time he might have been Johnny Appleseed. Bringing death in order to preserve life. A Gary Cooper enfranchised to perform a necessary, but awful task. And though he is only a man, we can see the responsibility of the heavy burden he carries, in his face. We also see his kindness: he is accompanied only by a dog, to whom he speaks, pouring out his compassion.

He carries with him a filtration pack, like a rucksack on his back. Connected to it by a pair of thin hoses is a plastic breather mask (clear, transparent, like a clothing baggie a child might play with). This he wears when he locates, and enters, a possibly contaminated crypt. It keeps any possible

airborne virus from contaminating him.  As long as he smashes the
mechanisms, and does not open the pods, he is safe.

He discovers a lost crypt, buried in the hillside.  He
blasts it open, goes inside, and begins smashing the mechanisms
of the pods.  Then, a horrifying discovery.  One pod, with the
nameplate Maria Cuevos, is empty.  Not ruined, not smashed, not
gone foul over the years.  It has malfunctioned only recently,
and opened.  It has released its occupant.  He follows the
footprints in the dust of the crypt, to a passage through which
Maria has gained escape from the cryonic chamber.

He tracks her, and quickly finds her, that night, huddled
on the hillside, trying to keep warm at a small fire.

For the first time he has to be a murderer.  It was easy
for him to rationalize the destruction of mechanical systems,
because the people inside would not suffer.  They would just
die in their decades-long sleep.  But this is a live woman, a
breathing human being.

She, of course, has no idea what year it is, what has
happened to the human race...and what danger he presents to
her new life.

He cannot bring himself simply to kill her on the spot.
She is sweet, ingenuous, and pretty.  She asks him for help.
She is like a new-born child, looking for protection.

He wears his mask throughout the time they spend together,
and because he has been a lonely man, doing a lonely and awful

ELLISON / 4

job, he succumbs to her decency and helplessness. They fall in love. The story moves quickly, and a day later it becomes apparent that they will become lovers.

In the final moment of the segment, they walk hand-in-hand toward the ridge, and as CAMERA BEGINS TO PULL BACK AND BACK, they vanish over the rise. A moment later we hear a shocking sound: a single gunshot.

CAMERA KEEPS PULLING BACK and as the angle widens we see his face mask placed carefully on a rock. And then...

A second shot.

Love, and responsibility, and caring. At the final, terrible, human moment.

HARLAN ELLISON® has been characterized by *The New York Times Book Review* as having "the spellbinding quality of a great nonstop talker, with a cultural warehouse for a mind." *The Los Angeles Times* suggested, "It's long past time for Harlan Ellison to be awarded the title: 20th century Lewis Carroll." And the *Washington Post Book World* said simply, "One of the great living American short story writers."

He has written or edited 76 books; more than 1700 stories, essays, articles, and newspaper columns; two dozen teleplays, for which he received the Writers Guild of America most outstanding teleplay award for solo work an unprecedented four times; and a dozen movies. *Publishers Weekly* called him "Highly Intellectual." (Ellison's response: "Who, Me?"). He won the Mystery Writers of America Edgar Allan Poe award twice, the Horror Writers Association Bram Stoker award six times (including The Lifetime Achievement Award in 1996), the Nebula award of the Science Fiction Writers of America four times, the Hugo (World Convention Achievement award) 8 ½ times, and received the Silver Pen for Journalism from P.E.N. Not to mention the World Fantasy Award; the British Fantasy Award; the American Mystery Award; plus two Audie Awards and two Grammy nominations for Spoken Word recordings.

He created great fantasies for the 1985 CBS revival of *The Twilight Zone* (including Danny Kaye's final performance) and *The Outer Limits*, traveled with The Rolling Stones; marched with Martin Luther King from Selma to Montgomery; created roles for Buster Keaton, Wally Cox, Gloria Swanson, and nearly 100 other stars on *Burke's Law*; ran with a kid gang in Brooklyn's Red Hook to get background for his first novel; covered race riots in Chicago's "back of the yards" with the late James Baldwin; sang with, and dined with, Maurice Chevalier; once stood off the son of the Detroit Mafia kingpin with a Remington XP-l00 pistol-rifle, while wearing nothing but a bath towel; sued Paramount and ABC-TV for plagiarism and won $337,000. His most recent legal victory, in protection of copyright against global Internet piracy of writers' work, in May of 2004—a four-year-long litigation against AOL et al.—has resulted in revolutionizing protection of creative properties on the web. (As promised, he has repaid hundreds of contributions [totaling $50,000] from the KICK Internet Piracy support fund.) But the bottom line, as voiced by *Booklist*, is this: "One thing for sure: the man can write."

He lives with his wife, Susan, inside The Lost Aztec Temple of Mars, in Los Angeles.

# CHRONOLOGY OF BOOKS BY
# HARLAN ELLISON®
## 1958 – 2014

**RETROSPECTIVES:**

ALONE AGAINST TOMORROW: *A 10-Year Survey* [1971]

THE ESSENTIAL ELLISON: *A 35-Year Retrospective*
(edited by Terry Dowling, with Richard Delap & Gil Lamont)
[1987]

THE ESSENTIAL ELLISON: *A 50-Year Retrospective*
(edited by Terry Dowling) [2001]

UNREPENTANT: *A Celebration of the Writing of
Harlan Ellison* (edited by Robert T. Garcia) [2010]

**OMNIBUS VOLUMES:**

THE FANTASIES OF HARLAN ELLISON [1979]

DREAMS WITH SHARP TEETH [1991]

THE GLASS TEAT & THE OTHER GLASS TEAT [2011]

**GRAPHIC NOVELS:**

DEMON WITH A GLASS HAND
(adaptation with Marshall Rogers) [1986]

NIGHT AND THE ENEMY
(adaptation with Ken Steacy) [1987]

VIC AND BLOOD: *The Chronicles of a Boy and His Dog*
(adaptation by Richard Corben) [1989]

HARLAN ELLISON'S DREAM CORRIDOR, Volume One [1996]

VIC AND BLOOD: *The Continuing Adventures of a Boy and
His Dog* (adaptation by Richard Corben) [2003]

HARLAN ELLISON'S DREAM CORRIDOR, Volume Two [2007]

PHOENIX WITHOUT ASHES
(art by Alan Robinson, and John K. Snyder III) [2010/2011]

HARLAN ELLISON'S 7 AGAINST CHAOS
(art by Paul Chadwick and Ken Steacy) [2013]

**THE HARLAN ELLISON DISCOVERY SERIES:**

STORMTRACK by James Sutherland [1975]

AUTUMN ANGELS by Arthur Byron Cover [1975]

THE LIGHT AT THE END OF THE UNIVERSE
by Terry Carr [1976]

ISLANDS by Marta Randall [1976]

INVOLUTION OCEAN by Bruce Sterling [1978]

**NOVELS:**

WEB OF THE CITY [1958]

THE SOUND OF A SCYTHE [1960]

SPIDER KISS [1961]

**SHORT NOVELS:**

DOOMSMAN [1967]

ALL THE LIES THAT ARE MY LIFE [1980]

RUN FOR THE STARS [1991]

MEFISTO IN ONYX [1993]

**COLLABORATIONS:**

PARTNERS IN WONDER:
*Collaborations with 14 Other Wild Talents* [1971]

THE STARLOST: *Phoenix Without Ashes*
(with Edward Bryant) [1975]

MIND FIELDS:
*33 Stories Inspired by the Art of Jacek Yerka* [1994]

I HAVE NO MOUTH, AND I MUST SCREAM:
*The Interactive CD-Rom*
(Co-Designed with David Mullich and David Sears) [1995]

"REPENT, HARLEQUIN!" SAID THE TICKTOCKMAN
(rendered with paintings by Rick Berry) [1997]

2000$^X$ (Host and Creative Consultant
of National Public Radio episodic series) [2000–2001]

HARLAN ELLISON'S MORTAL DREADS
(dramatized by Robert Armin) [2012]

THE DISCARDED (with Josh Olson) [Forthcoming]

**AS EDITOR:**

DANGEROUS VISIONS [1967]

NIGHTSHADE & DAMNATIONS:
*The Finest Stories of Gerald Kersh* [1968]

AGAIN, DANGEROUS VISIONS [1972]

MEDEA: HARLAN'S WORLD [1985]

DANGEROUS VISIONS (The 35th Anniversary Edition) [2002]

JACQUES FUTRELLE'S
"THE THINKING MACHINE" STORIES [2003]

# CHRONOLOGY OF BOOKS BY
## HARLAN ELLISON®
### 1958 – 2014

**SHORT STORY COLLECTIONS:**

THE DEADLY STREETS [1958]

SEX GANG (as "Paul Merchant") [1959]

A TOUCH OF INFINITY [1960]

CHILDREN OF THE STREETS [1961]

GENTLEMAN JUNKIE
and Other Stories of the Hung-Up Generation [1961]

ELLISON WONDERLAND [1962]

PAINGOD and Other Delusions [1965]

I HAVE NO MOUTH & I MUST SCREAM [1967]

FROM THE LAND OF FEAR [1967]

LOVE AIN'T NOTHING BUT SEX MISSPELLED [1968]

THE BEAST THAT SHOUTED LOVE
AT THE HEART OF THE WORLD [1969]

OVER THE EDGE [1970]

ALL THE SOUNDS OF FEAR
(British publication only) [1973]

DE HELDEN VAN DE HIGHWAY
(Dutch publication only) [1973]

APPROACHING OBLIVION [1974]

THE TIME OF THE EYE (British publication only) [1974]

DEATHBIRD STORIES [1975]

NO DOORS, NO WINDOWS [1975]

HOE KAN IK SCHREEUWEN ZONDER MOND
(Dutch publication only) [1977]

STRANGE WINE [1978]

SHATTERDAY [1980]

STALKING THE NIGHTMARE [1982]

ANGRY CANDY [1988]

ENSAMVÄRK (Swedish publication only) [1992]

JOKES WITHOUT PUNCHLINES [1995]

ВСЕ ЗВУКИ СТРАХА (ALL FEARFUL SOUNDS)
(Unauthorized Russian publication only) [1997]

THE WORLDS OF HARLAN ELLISON
(Authorized Russian publication only) [1997]

SLIPPAGE: Precariously Poised, Previously Uncollected Stories
[1997]

KOLETIS, KES KUULUTAS ARMASTUST MAAILMA SLIDAMES
(Estonian publication only) [1999]

LA MACHINE AUX YEUX BLEUS
(French publication only) [2001]

TROUBLEMAKERS [2001]

PTAK ŚMIERCI (THE BEST OF HARLAN ELLISON)
(Polish publication only) [2003]

DEATHBIRD STORIES (expanded edition) [2011]

PULLING A TRAIN [2012]

GETTING IN THE WIND [2012]

**NON-FICTION & ESSAYS:**

MEMOS FROM PURGATORY [1961]

THE GLASS TEAT: Essays of Opinion on Television [1970]

THE OTHER GLASS TEAT:
Further Essays of Opinion on Television [1975]

THE BOOK OF ELLISON
(edited by Andrew Porter) [1978]

SLEEPLESS NIGHTS IN THE PROCRUSTEAN BED
(edited by Marty Clark) [1984]

AN EDGE IN MY VOICE [1985]

HARLAN ELLISON'S WATCHING [1989]

THE HARLAN ELLISON HORNBOOK [1990]

BUGF#CK! The Useless Wit & Wisdom of Harlan Ellison
(edited by Arnie Fenner) [2011]

# CHRONOLOGY OF BOOKS BY
# HARLAN ELLISON®
## 1958 – 2014

**SCREENPLAYS & SUCHLIKE:**

THE ILLUSTRATED HARLAN ELLISON
(edited by Byron Preiss) [1978]

HARLAN ELLISON'S MOVIE [1990]

I, ROBOT: THE ILLUSTRATED SCREENPLAY
(based on Isaac Asimov's story-cycle) [1994]

THE CITY ON THE EDGE OF FOREVER [1996]

**MOTION PICTURE (DOCUMENTARY):**

DREAMS WITH SHARP TEETH (A Film About Harlan Ellison
produced and directed by Erik Nelson) [2009]

**ON THE ROAD WITH HARLAN ELLISON:**

ON THE ROAD WITH HARLAN ELLISON (Vol. One)
[1983/2001]

ON THE ROAD WITH HARLAN ELLISON (Vol. Two) [2004]

ON THE ROAD WITH HARLAN ELLISON (Vol. Three) [2007]

ON THE ROAD WITH HARLAN ELLISON:
HIS LAST BIG CON (Vol. Five) [2011]

ON THE ROAD WITH HARLAN ELLISON:
THE GRAND MASTER EDITION (Vol. Six) [2012]

**AUDIOBOOKS:**

THE VOICE FROM THE EDGE: I HAVE NO MOUTH, AND I
MUST SCREAM (Vol. One) [1999]

THE VOICE FROM THE EDGE: MIDNIGHT IN THE SUNKEN
CATHEDRAL (Vol. Two) [2001]

RUN FOR THE STARS [2005]

THE VOICE FROM THE EDGE: PRETTY MAGGIE MONEYEYES
(Vol. Three) [2009]

THE VOICE FROM THE EDGE: THE DEATHBIRD & OTHER
STORIES (Vol. Four) [2011]

THE VOICE FROM THE EDGE: SHATTERDAY
& OTHER STORIES (Vol. Five) [2011]

**THE WHITE WOLF SERIES:**

EDGEWORKS 1: OVER THE EDGE
& AN EDGE IN MY VOICE [1996]

EDGEWORKS 2: SPIDER KISS
& STALKING THE NIGHTMARE [1996]

EDGEWORKS 3: THE HARLAN ELLISON HORNBOOK &
HARLAN ELLISON'S MOVIE [1997]

EDGEWORKS 4: LOVE AIN'T NOTHING BUT SEX MISSPELLED
& THE BEAST THAT SHOUTED LOVE AT THE HEART OF THE
WORLD [1997]

**EDGEWORKS ABBEY OFFERINGS**
**(Edited by Jason Davis):**

BRAIN MOVIES: THE ORIGINAL TELEPLAYS OF
HARLAN ELLISON (Vol. One) [2011]

BRAIN MOVIES: THE ORIGINAL TELEPLAYS OF
HARLAN ELLISON (Vol. Two) [2011]

HARLAN 101: ENCOUNTERING ELLISON [2011]

THE SOUND OF A SCYTHE *and 3 Brilliant Novellas* [2011]

ROUGH BEASTS: *Seventeen Stories
Written Before I Got Up To Speed* [2012]

NONE OF THE ABOVE [2012]

BRAIN MOVIES: THE ORIGINAL TELEPLAYS OF
HARLAN ELLISON (Vol. Three) [2013]

BRAIN MOVIES: THE ORIGINAL TELEPLAYS OF
HARLAN ELLISON (Vol. Four) [2013]

BRAIN MOVIES: THE ORIGINAL TELEPLAYS OF
HARLAN ELLISON (Vol. Five) [2013]

HONORABLE WHOREDOM AT A PENNY A WORD [2013]

AGAIN, HONORABLE WHOREDOM AT A PENNY A WORD
[2014]

BRAIN MOVIES: THE ORIGINAL TELEPLAYS OF
HARLAN ELLISON (Vol. Six) [2014]

HARLAN ELLISON'S ENDLESSLY WATCHING [2014]

8 IN 80 BY ELLISON (guest edited by Susan Ellison) [2014]

Made in the USA
Charleston, SC
29 July 2016